ANTHONY FRISELL

THE
TENOR VOICE

A Personal Guide to
Acquiring a Superior Singing Technique

An expanded and updated edition

Branden Publishing Company
IPL Series
www.brandenbooks.com
Boston

Library of Congress Cataloging-in-Publication Data

Frisell, Anthony.
 The Tenor voice : a personal guide to acquiring a superior singing technique / Anthony
Frisell. -- Expanded and updated ed.
     p. cm.
"First English printing: Bruce Humphries, 1964."
ISBN-13: 978-0-8283-2183-9 (pbk. : alk. paper)
 1. Singing--Instruction and study.
 2. Tenors (Singers)--Training of.
 I. Title.

MT820.F865 2007
783.8'7143--dc22

2007000584

www.brandenbooks.com
IPL Series
Branden Publishing Company
PO Box 812094
Wellesley MA 02482

This book was written in appreciation
of the pleasure and personal fulfillment
I have experienced
during a lifetime of involvement
with the art of singing and teaching singers

CONTENTS

Ramp, ● Special exercises for structuring the Passaggio tones, ● Training the tongue and soft palate to assume their proper positions and behavioral movements, ● The E♭ "switch-over", Fulcrum Tone", ● The transportable power of the chest voice, ● Ascending vocal movement, ● The *"Bari-Tenors"* of recent times, ● Getting ready to sing after vocalization, ● The classic songs and arias of the Seventeenth and Eighteenth Centuries, ● The nature and important function of the impingement or *"hookup points"* that line the vocal tract, ● The*"Witch's Voice", or voce di strega* , ● The *"mezzo-falso"* or *"mixed-voice "*, ● Cracking a tone, ● The "inverted tone", ● The "Vocal Platform", ● The raw sound of the a (ah) vowel, when pronounced, in a fully open-throat manner like the word **"at",** ● The "hollow u (oo) vowel", and how it relates to perfecting the *passaggio*, or registers' break tones, ● Hollow o (oh) vowel exercises, ● *Giorgio Roncone's* amazing discovery concerning the u (oo) vowel, ● *Giovanni Sbriglia's "piccolo ",* or *"tiny"* u (oo) vowel, ● The *"Gathered Voice",* and The Head Voice Ramp, ● The tongue, ● The consonants, ● The lips and facial muscles.

Are you in earnest? Seize this very minute, What you can do, or dream you can—begin it! Boldness has genius, power, and magic in it. Only engage and then the mind grows heated, Begin and then the work will be completed.

Johann Wolfgang von Goethe—
Born August 28, 1749 in Frankfurt (am main), Germany

CHAPTER ONE

The Mental Image Approach

To train the singing voice one must establish a system of vocal exercises, however, because of the physiological location of the vocal organ these exercises cannot be applied in a direct manner, such as one would do to exercise the arms or legs. Therefore, vocal exercises must be applied *indirectly,* through mental concepts. We call this method the *mental image approach.*

The beginner's mental image of his voice has such a critical influence upon what he produces vocally that establishing correct mental concepts is paramount. For example, if a beginner's voice is *incorrectly* classified as a baritone, which is frequently the case with a "heavier" voice tenor, or a tenor with absolutely no "head voice" development, he will often make a conscious effort to produce vocal qualities and characteristics which he associates with the baritone voice, thereby denying the appropriate qualities and developmental needs of his own "natural" tenor voice. The first step in correcting the problem is to change the student's mental concepts of his voice.

By correctly applying the rules set forth in the mental image control theory, a formula can be had for developing the singing voice. The formula will contain all the basic rudiments that are required, and include the ideals of perfection which represent the finished art of the vocal instrument. This method allows for all changes necessary for improving the voice throughout the entire course of training. It also gives the student guiding rules, so he can compare each stage of his vocal development with the ideal.

Although it is hoped that the text is explicit, the nature of signing requires that the voice student hear the best of live performances, so that a more complete understanding of the standards of the art may be gained. There are many who feel that present-day singers are below par and unworthy of emulation, therefore students should be rather selective and seek out the best singers of his time. Technical criticism should be directed at the way singers use their voices and not at the voice itself, since singers are not equally endowed with great voices or *inherent singing talent.*

By approaching training with a predetermined mental image, the beginner has an outline of what is expected of him in order to attain professional status. Present-day singers are expected to be more vocally polished at their initial professional debut than singers of the past, since their performance will be compared with some particular artist of a currently popular recording. To add to their difficulties there are practically no small theaters in which to gain professional experience. Singers of the past had the advantage of testing themselves in small theaters, thereby smoothing out their technical problems, long before submitting themselves to the judgment of audiences in the major theaters. The availability so many CD recordings of famous singers is another thorn in the side of the beginner; since he is always being compared to the way "*So-and-so* sang it on records." Very few students realize that the "near perfection" standards of current recordings are often mainly due to feats of engineering skill.

Many present-day singers could well be taken to task for their attitude toward continued study of their vocal technique, after they have made their professional debuts. Most think that the few years they have studied has prepared them for any role in the repertory and that they are free from further vocal work. Nothing could be further from the truth—maintaining high vocal standards is a lifetime study. The voice is always changing, even though the technique be correct. It should be explicitly understood that the *singing voice is always in a process of growing change.* To assure that the correct direction is taken when these changes occur, the technique must possess certain fixed rules of guidance which allow for changes and still permit the singer to continue performing. The rules of the *vocal image control theory* must be very tangible! The highest standard attainable will depend completely upon what the singer technically conceives of as being correct. With continual use, some vocal experiences prove beneficial and others undesirable. By comparing good and bad functions, and selecting those which the correct mental image indicates are preferable, the singer may progresses from one state of vocal efficiency to a better one.

Fixed Rules

Certain *fixed rules* form the basis for the correct mental image.

The Vowels

Correct formation of the five so-called classic Italian vowels *u (oo), i (ee), e (eh), o (oh) and a (ah),* is the most basic and essential of vocal functions, and the singer's only reliable method of checking himself against bad singing habits. The manner in which *native Italians* pronounce the five vowels, purely and free of diphthongs, should be used for all exercises in this manual. Distorted vowels blur the words of a musical piece and deny the singer communication with his listeners. But more importantly, the vowels control the muscles of the vocal organ, and when they are not produced correctly, they deny beauty of tone and vocal control. Even if the language in which a singer is singing is foreign to his audience, the lack of vowel clarity soon becomes apparent in a monotony of tonal colors. From the very beginning of study, the singer must be determined *not* to sacrifice the purity of the vowel to attain the pitch, or tonal effect, or he will always be limited by those compromises. Each of the five vowels must be mastered in its purest form throughout the entire vocal range.

Control

Control, which means *muscular* control, cannot be over emphasized because no matter what quality of sound or extension of range is achieved, without control it is unreliable. Until complete control is established the singer can never pass to a state of proficiency where the technique becomes *second-nature.* Mastery over all the dynamics, a full range, flexibility, and shading of tones permits artistic interpretation. All are the results of control.

Musicianship

Musicianship, which is of major importance, is frequently neglected or passed over lightly. A singer must become familiar with the rudiments of music and acquire some ability to play a musical instrument, preferably the piano. Also, the nature of what is musical in vocal production, and what factors make the singing voice a musical instrument, should be carefully studied and cultivated. The tenor must be particularly alert to musical theory because in ensemble singing he will be expected to harmonize with the voices of other soloists. The goal of all singers should be the attainment of precise intonation, musical sensitivity, an accurate sense of pitch and legato, and all patterns necessary for a musical vocal production.

A singer must understand that what is necessary for vocal improvement is *change,* and that this change is the result of what he technically perceives to be better. Without change he can only perpetuate his present vocal faults. In the search for vocal improvement there is always varied opinions of what is right and wrong, and the student can easily become confused and frustrated. It is always wise to pay attention to criticism, consider the sources of opinions, then permit the passing of time for testing suggested theories. Remember that vocal progress is always reflected in ease of production, the overcoming of difficulties, and a positive response from your listeners.

The "Science of Voice" Advocates

A matter which deserves mention, even though it is opposed to the simplicity of the *mental image control theory*, is the growing popularity to investigate the anatomical aspects of voice production, commonly referred to as the *"science of voice."* The practice of the *Science Of Voice* advocates is to directly manipulate parts of the vocal apparatus itself, with their fingers, in the hope of strengthening and extending the vocal range, and getting "control of the voice". For example, some of them attempt to control the actions of the tongue with a "tongue depressor". The only correct way to control the tongue, is to *not try* to control it at all, but to develop the two vocal registers, employing pure vowels, which correctly and precisely, and most importantly, *musically* control the proper functions of the tongue. Other advocates of the *Science Of Voice* training method depress the larynx with their thumb and forefingers. Those teachers who practice these methods of so-called voice training attract their students by promising them a supposed *faster method* of voice development. The scientific speedy-method always fails.

Medically speaking, science has made much progress in treating the victims of speech defects. However, as a method of training the singer voice, it is *useless.*

Any student who submits his voice to this method of training should be made aware that he is risking permanent damage of his vocal organ. Few of the great singers of the past even knew the names given to the parts of the singing voice, much less employed them in a method of instruction. The less known in this direction, the sooner the singer will learn to depend on, and utilize mental concepts, which stimulate musical feelings and simplify, not complicate his task.

These aforementioned rules, which represent a correct mental image, when applied to any well used singing voice will serve to confirm what is already in proper function. For the beginner, they will guide him to attaining a reliable vocal technique. For the advanced, professional singer, they may serve as a reminder of the standard to maintain. They are, however, only a partial guide for developing a singing voice, and must be extended into a more specific direction—this being the complete understanding of the two *vocal registers.*

CHAPTER TWO

Identifying the Vocal Registers

To acquire a reliable vocal technique a student must have clear and precise concepts to guide him. The functions of the vocal registers help to serve that purpose. The vocal registers allow for definite rules of vocal control which are based upon the consistent *muscular patterns* of responses of the vocal organ itself. They are very specific. Any other means of obtaining a correct vocal production, when based solely on the quality and range of a beginner's voice, generally ends in failure.

The human voice is capable of producing many varieties of sound which have contrasting characteristics. To base the vocal technique on any particular sound quality is too vague a method because the tonal qualities used by the average beginner are generally *imitated,* and often chosen to compensate for his vocal limitations and to please his temperament. The singer who knows what the fully developed vocal registers are capable of possesses a *definite image* of the ideal vocal state toward which he must strive.

Defining the Vocal Registers

A vocal register is a group of tones with harmonious qualities produced by one muscular mechanism, and differs from another contrasting muscular mechanism of equally harmonious qualities, timber and strength. *To master the art of refined singing one must know the functions of the two vocal registers and develop them so they operate together as a single muscular unit of quality and strength throughout the entire vocal range.* There are other factors to consider, however, they are mainly matters of vowel purity/or distortion, throat constrictions, and other irregularities of tone production. They may become corrected, along with the development and understanding of usage, of the vocal registers themselves.

There are but two vocal registers. Within the complete range of the tenor voice, minor mechanical variations have been observed and it has often been *incorrectly* theorized that there are three or four registers. This is false, and the fallacy of the three, or four registers theory can be understood when the two registers are properly developed and united.

A permanent antagonism exists between the two vocal registers

One of the most important and generally overlooked aspects concerning the two vocal registers is that *they are permanently antagonistic toward each other*. This antagonism remains in operation from the beginning phase of vocal training *(when the voice is unstructured)*, until the final phase of development. Because of this antagonism it is therefore difficult and time-consuming to subjugate the registers to a training program of muscular structuring. The accomplishment is generally known as the muscular "harmonizing of the registers". It is this same, initial state of antagonism which, when properly understood and used to advantage, gives the superior singing instrument its remarkable controls and qualities. These two major muscular systems, in their *antagonistic* state, strongly resist the singer's efforts to maintain control over their separate, dynamic actions, denying him his wish to muscularly unify all the tones of his complete singing range. Correct structuring imposes rules upon these two antagonistic muscular systems, so they *will* come to function as a single unit throughout the vocal range, thereby granting the singer the necessary muscular controls over his instrument. In this way, the singing instrument functions as a *synergism.*

Before presenting additional ideas on how and what these two registers contribute to the structuring process, it is necessary to establish exactly where, in the singer's total range of vocal tones, the critical *point of division* which separates them is *permanently* located.

    Figure No. 1 (below), shows the position of the tenor's Registers' Break, situated between E♮ and F♮ above middle C. All tones below En above middle C belong to the *Lower Muscular System,* the E♮ included. This muscular system is generally known as the *Chest Register.* From F♮ above middle C, and upward, all tones belong to the *Upper Register,* the F♮ included. This muscular system is generally known as the *Head Register.* The location of the *Registers' Break* remains in this permanently fixed

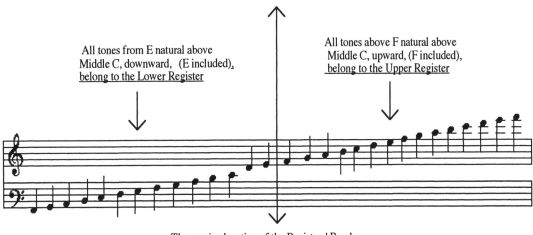

All tones from E natural above
Middle C, downward, (E included),
belong to the Lower Register

All tones above F natural above
Middle C, upward, (F included),
belong to the Upper Register

The precise location of the Registers' Break,
between E and F natural, above Middle C

position for all vocal categories, as will be explained in greater detail.

The permanent location of the "registers' break"

    The point of division between the two vocal registers is most frequently referred to as the "registers' break". It is a natural, permanent factor of singing voices of all vocal categories. It has been termed a "breaking point" because, when the untrained singer attempts to sing vocal phrases, or execute vocal scales that cross this critical area of his complete range, the muscles of the two registers, which meet between E♮ and F♮ above middle C, most frequently *"break"* apart, react antagonistically toward each other, and refuse to cooperate in the production of satisfactory musical tone.

    But he inherent antagonism which exists between the two vocal registers *can* be permanently altered through selected exercises, causing them to interact in a cooperative team- effort, which allows for superior singing. However, the point of division remains forever located at its original place in the singer's vocal range. What changes is the behavior of the muscles that lie on either side of the "break point". In this new, cooperative state, they allow the singer to sing in the "break area" with complete control of the dynamics, from soft to loud and back again to soft, and to "pronounce" the five vowels *(u, i, e, o, and a)* purely.

The vocal "passaggio"

    Several tones located *below* the register's break and several *above* it represent an area of all singers' vocal range which presents great difficulties in singing with precise intonation, a full range of dynamics, and pure vowels. This area is frequently referred to as the vocal *"passaggio",* an Italian word which means *passageway*. It is critical for all singers to muscularly structure all the passaggio tones to a state of perfection in order to achieve a superior standard of vocal production, but especially so for tenors, since they must sing in *passaggio area* for a greater length of time than all other male singers. It takes many years of hard work to bring the *passaggio* tones to a state of perfection.

During that time, the student-singer *can not* attain the kind of high quality, professional vocal sounds he desires, however, he is obliged to tolerate these unattractive, unprofessional, temporary sounds, in order to eventually become a professional singer.

Throughout this manual, many references will be made to the problems which the *passaggio* presents to all singers, and the various exercises necessary to overcome them.

Some basic characteristics and terms that are often applied to the two vocal registers

Both vocal registers contribute inherent muscular actions and tonal *timbres* to the singing instrument. These *muscular actions* and *timbres* provoke descriptions of the vocal sounds they produce, based upon subjective impressions.

The Lower Register

The vocal sounds of the lower register's range of tones *(the "chest voice")* are often referred to as "resonance" or "vocal solidity" factors. This register contributes the basic power factor *("vocal projection" in the theater).* to the singing instrument. Some familiar terms that attempt to describe the variety of *tonal timbres* contributed by the lower register are: "ring", "bite", "core", "solidity", "bright" and "resonance". The term "resonance" is incorrectly applied, as it correctly describes the presence of the *vibrato* action of the vocal cords. The vocal sounds of singing are the result of the vibrating action of the vocal cords, set into vibratory motion by "breath pressure" being applied to them, which in turn produces the prolongation of sound produced by sympathetic vibrations known as "tone". The *vibrato action* of the vocal cords *is a correct and desired function of the vocal instrument.*

The Upper Register

The vocal sounds of the tenor's upper register's range of tones *(the "head voice")* or "falsetto" register are most often referred to as "sweet" or "ethereal" or "soprano-like", and its muscular actions contribute beauty of vocal tone, flexibility of control, and vocal shading. Some of the terms applied to its range of tones are: "the dark voice", "the juvenile voice", "the false voice" "the unconnected voice", "the amateur voice" and the "thin register".

Paradoxically, one set of the five singing vowels can be produced in the lower register, maintaining the sounds and muscular characteristics indigenous to that register, while another set of the five vowels can be produced in the upper register's vowels, maintaining the sounds and muscular characteristics indigenous to that register. Yet, when the singer attempts to combine the basic sounds and muscular actions of the lower register's vowels with those of the upper register's, on any given tone or groups of tones, it is impossible to achieve a match or "blend" of the registers' muscular actions and sounds without restructuring the complete vocal range . Only when their muscular actions have been "blended" will they allow for a mutual exchange of their separate qualities and muscular actions.

This refusal, by the registers, to exchange their basic muscular actions and tonal qualities is a tangible and graphic demonstration of the undeniable division between these two, major muscular systems. This conflict is acknowledged by the international community of vocal musicologists. Many technique books have been written which discuss the subject of the vocal registers, the mystifying registers' break which separates them, and the difficulty the registers' break presents, when the singer executes an extended vocal scale, either ascending or descending, into the break area with the intention of unifying all the tonal qualities and muscular actions of each and every one of the scale's tones. It has seldom been stated, however, that the problems caused by the registers' break are the same factors which, when understood, can be used advantageously as the tools for correctly structuring a superior vocal instrument.

The purpose of this manual is to explain and clarify the antagonisms of the two registers, and further, to outline the precise methods of using them in a reliable and consistent vocal structuring program.

When a tenor attempts to sing phrases or exercise-scales that ascend into the area of the registers' break, using the a (ah) vowel, and a reasonably strong volume, *unless* that area has been correctly restructured, he is *denied* the attainment of correctly functioning, beautiful tones in that area, plus the tones situated just above the *passaggio.* He is forced to compromise their quality and control. This compromise results in impure vowels, and harsh, unmusical tones. This unsatisfactory vocal condition may be referred to as a state of "uncoordinated vocal registers", meaning the singer has *not* managed to circumvent the basic antagonism that exists between the two registers. The singer, with this vocal condition, usually possesses a voice with strong, thick lower and middle range tones, a few faulty, barely accessible tones in the registers' break area, and above the registers' break area, forced, unmusical tones that are "weak", "uncoordinated" and "unmatched" in tonal quality to the lower part of his range. This singer's upper tones are disadvantageously restricted by the negative muscular controls of the chest voice and are in need of help from the head voice muscles.

In order to overcome these unavoidable vocal limitations that exist between the two registers, it is necessary for the singer to train these antagonistic registers toward a state of harmony. Expressed in other words, *the muscular controls of the two separate vocal registers must be blended*, or better said, "muscularly restructured" so that they function *as one*, both in muscular action and tonal quality, throughout the singer's complete range.

Because there exist so many conflicting muscular actions, tonal varieties and variations of physical sensations operating between these two major muscular systems, which cause them to *permanently react antagonistically toward each other,* the controversial question always arises as to what, precisely, about these two registers is *"accurate" and/or "inaccurate"*, where superior singing is concerned? Therefore, we must establish a ruling principle as a foundation for correct development.

A ruling principle

The conflicting muscular responses that occur between the two vocal registers, when attempting to produce pure, superior vocal tone and clearly pronounced vowels throughout the entire vocal range, represent the natural muscular responses of the both vocal registers to the energy of the breath tension, or motor force that must be applied to them, in order to produce basic pitch and to achieve developmental goals.

We can better understand the antagonistic nature of the two registers by thinking of their basic response to each other as a form of tug-of-war, each register struggling for dominance over the other. Where singing is concerned, the lower register, however, has many advantages, although negative, over the weaker upper register. The lower register is generally the stronger of the two, at the onset of vocal training.

There are several factors that contribute to the inherent dominance of the lower register over the upper register.

l. The muscles that produce the *lower register's tones* are inherently larger than those of the head voice register. However, tenor voices, when properly structured must possess more *head tones* than *chest tones*. But the chest voice must still contribute certain indispensable muscular controls to the fully developed singing voice, since without them, the singer's entire range would "closed down" *(more about this in detail, later)*.

2. Most training programs erroneously apply their basic exercises to the bottom of the singer's vocal range, where the lower register is most powerful. This gives the lower register *yet another negative advantage* over the inherently weaker upper register, in winning the tug-of-war between the registers.

3. Singers, or singer and teacher working together, are often volume-conscious, impatiently seeking the quick attainment of "resonant, powerful, professional-sounding tones". They fail to consider the developmental attributes of the upper register's muscular controls, which are more subtle, and can only be invoked and strengthened by the use of upper register's soft tonal dynamics. These upper registers' muscular controls take much longer to develop, and longer to reveal their true tonal qualities and muscular contributions than do the readily available chest tones. The valuable, long-range benefits derived from cultivating the softer and subtler *(but in no way weaker, when fully developed)*, muscular controls of the upper register are frequently neglected by the "volume-conscious, quick-results student." This is because, the falsetto muscles, in their earlier phase of development, produce only "thin", "non-resonant" tonal qualities that are easily misunderstood as being "false" and unrelated to the advanced, full-volume, "legitimate" performing voice.

The full worth of the first falsetto sounds, produced by the beginner, are misleading. Interpreting their true value, as they progress in strength and yield benefits to the singer, and rendering judgments regarding their quality of tone, should be *reserved for expert ears.*

Despite the inherent dominance of the lower register, the singer or voice teacher, armed with accurate, specialized knowledge, can play a major role in deciding which of the two vocal registers will emerge as the dominant register.

Resolving the conflict between the two vocal registers can be accomplished, in part, by favoring the upper register. In the past, most vocal training programs utilized specialized exercises that gave *preference to the upper register's development*, with the intent of making *its* muscular controls the dominating controls of the singer's complete vocal range. This dominance in no way excludes the brilliance and power of the lower register, but rather assures that its brilliance and power are applied *safely*, since the chest voice, *when operating without the collaboration of the upper register,* can be damaging to the singing voice.

During early training, the muscular activities of the lower register must be relegated to a *temporarily* passive and *subordinate* role. Many singers and teachers avoid a program of "head voice", or "falsetto" training because falsetto sounds produced during the building process *are unfamiliar,* when compared to the sounds of the chest voice, and, to most individuals, they appear remote and confusing. This occurs because the various "sound" aspects of the developing falsetto voice and the positive changes they produce upon the developing singing voice *have not been heard* in most training studios for several decades, and *have not*, therefore, been passed down to present-day vocal teachers. This has set in motion an unfortunate downward spiral in the quality of present-day singing.

At the beginning of this *head-voice-training-program*, the singer is generally dealing with underdeveloped muscular conditions in both the upper and lower registers, which are incapable of producing the beautiful, highly-controlled tones of the advanced vocal state. This advanced vocal state can only be attained over a long period of time, through much discipline and the application of superior technical knowledge. One of the most blatant faults of contemporary training occurs when teachers fail to make allowances for the "raw", "crude", almost uncontrollable vocal sounds that most beginners must produce during the early phases of training. Most teachers instead quickly attempt to obtain "polished", "beautiful", and highly-controlled vocal sounds from their students, which can only be produced by advanced professionals. For an untrained voice to progress from the crude vocal sounds of *an amateur* to the beautiful and highly-controlled vocal sounds of *a professional* is a matter of correct muscular

Anthony Frisell—14

development of the entire vocal instrument. *It is not* a matter of the singer comprehending the "esthetics, beauty, and subtleties of refined singing", which some teachers wrongly assume, or imitating a famous artist of the day. Professional singers, too, are guilty of hindering beginners, in their failure to give testimonies of the earlier, less ideal stages of their voices, when they, too, *could not* produce controlled beautiful tones. In that way, they must be considered *silent partners* in the conspiracy of ruinous vocal training methods being practiced today, which do not allow the beginning singer his individual rate of vocal development.

In the untrained voice, the two registers *do not* function harmoniously with each other. In this state, the singer possesses a limited vocal range, unclear, "muddy" vowels, and many muscular conflicts and tonal inconsistencies. The lower register produces sounds that are thick and unmusical. When scales and vocal phrases are tried, the voice responds in a cumbersome manner. When the male singer ascends a vocal scale, the tones of the lower register reach a point of encounter with the weaker, thinner tones of the upper register system, as these tones inherently exist, prior to proper development, and the voice generally fails.

Tenors, in an understandable attempt to extend the *"solidity factor"* of their lower vocal range upward, frequently force the action of the lower register past the *dividing point* of the registers. This immediately halts the process of correct structuring of the singing voice, and in some cases causes damage.

The first major step in the long process of properly structuring the singing voice is for the singer to begin performing a series of exercises that will permanently reduce the undesirable bulk and thickness of the lower register. With tenor voices, the "strong and resonant" sounds of the vibrato action are usually readily understood and easily evoked, because they are produced by the vocal cords and the inherently dominant lower register's muscles. This register willingly grants the male singer an ample number of "chest tones" which, for a while, are generally comfortable to produce. The difficulty, where correct vocal structuring is concerned, is to transport the strong, vibrant sounds of the *vibrato action* to the tones that are situated above the registers' break, which, in their initial underdeveloped state, are unrelated in quality and muscular action to the tones produced by the lower *(chest)* register. Only with advanced development will the tenor be able to add the power of the chest voice to the thinner, yet equally strong, passageway *(when fully restructured),* of the upper head voice tract.

The task, for all male singers, is to first strengthen their underdeveloped upper register tones, above the registers' break, and transport these upper tones' muscular control downward in the range, until they appear to have adopted the resonant, vibrant quality of the lower register, but without losing their initial beauty and the inherent muscular controls of the upper register. *Student-tenors are advised that, after exercising the tones of the head voice, they must rest their voice for a period of hours, or a full day, before trying the voice, to observe what influence the exercises have had upon it. This is a golden rule which must be adopted from the onset of vocal training.* The cultivation of the muscular controls of the weaker head voice register *must be fully* accomplished, if the voice is to produce superior singing, necessary for a major professional career. *Avoidance of this critical issue is a guarantee for vocal failure, usually sooner than later.*

The process of developing the muscular controls of the underdeveloped falsetto register is slow and difficult to achieve, but when successfully accomplished, it gives to the singer a much admired *seamless vocal scale.* For the singer, the reality of this *seamless vocal scale* is quite different from the perception of it, experienced by his listeners. They are led to believe that all the tones of his superior singer's range are produced with a single muscular system, when, in truth, advanced superior singing employs *separate teams* of muscular controls, over which the singer, during a long and tedious training period, has become the master.

The master-singer develops a method of muscular coordination which allows him to transfer vocal control from one "team" of muscles, which control a particular section of the vocal range, to the *next team* of muscular controls, to accomplish the smooth, consistent production of superior tone and pure vowels, with a particular vocal exercise, or vocal phrase. The selection of a particular team of muscles to handle the "work load" of an exercise or vocal phrase is always relative to the section of the vocal range, which the musical exercise or vocal phrase demands. The most important of the master-singer's skills is to accomplish the transfer of muscular control from one team to the next, at the critical *transfer-point* of registers' break, in such a smooth, imperceptible manner that to his listeners, his vocal range appears to be but one seamless scale. More information on this complex aspect of the vocal instrument and the discrepancies between what the listener hears and what the singer is "actually doing", will be presented later. The subject has been touched upon at this early part of the manual to start the reader thinking about the complexities of "playing" the singing instrument. Singing is too often thought of in somewhat passive terms, as if, after the voice has been fully developed, it could "sing itself".

The metamorphoses of the two vocal registers

The reason that most vocal training methods *fail* to develop superior vocal instruments for hopeful students is because the muscles of the registers are generally accepted in their original, undeveloped state, wherein superior tones and advanced muscular maneuvers are asked of him. The student is assigned a series of difficult, rote, meaningless scales to perform, (*usually employed the "dangerous open, chest register's a (ah) vowel)*, in the *blind hope* of meeting the rigorous demands of superior singing. The vocal instrument must be structured with great care, since every chosen exercise brings with it consequences, good or bad. At the onset of training, the undeveloped voice *is not complete* nor perfectly assembled in the throat, waiting for the student to merely learn how to play it. On the contrary, the vocal range is fragmented and the student finds it nearly impossible to coordinate the applications of the breath force with quality of tone, vowel purity and vocal movement.

All superior voices are "created" by muscular structuring, achieved by transforming the undeveloped muscles of the two vocal registers *(from whatever starting condition in which they present themselves)*, to a "new" state of structural existence, one that must conform to, and in time, satisfy all the demands of a large repertory of difficult vocal literature. In the beginning, this transformation is accomplished by executing a series of selected exercises which favor the development of the upper register, so that *it* becomes the dominant muscular system.

What becomes evident, during this slow *building process*, is that the muscles controlling the tones of the *upper register* begin to grow in strength, first, within their original boundaries, and then, they can be transported physically *(not merely esthetically)*, downward in the vocal range, and made to overlap *all the tones* of the lower register.

Exercises will be presented which facilitate this desired downward "stretching" of the upper register's influences, until they the upper registers' muscular controls envelop all the tones of the lower or chest register. Once this has been accomplished *(this often takes years)*, the lower registers tones become restructured, and submit to the muscular controls of the upper register, which eventually dominate *all the tones of the singer' complete range.*

However, the upper register's controls <u>are not</u> sufficient in and of themselves to accomplish all the vocal tasks of the singing instrument, nor can they alone grant beauty and control of tone. They require the full and unique participation of the lower register's muscles to do so. This fact must be well noted, since many singers who embark upon a "falsetto" voice training program often feel they are free from all future involvement with the "thick" and "cumbersome" chest voice. Nothing could be further from the truth, and when the controls of the chest voice are denied, the result is always unattractive and unprofessional singing.

During the transformation of the upper register's muscles to a state of dominance, the process *automatically imposes a corresponding transformation of all the tones of the lower register.* In proportion to the ongoing development of all upper register tones, the corresponding *tones of the chest voice automatically and undeniably begin shrinking, and reducing their "weight" and "thickness"*. As a result of this metamorphosing process, the tones of the antagonistic chest voice are forced to subjugate themselves to the developing falsetto's muscular control, and begin to willingly participate in a "team effort" to accomplish the task of singing. During this phase, the developing voice goes through many frustrating periods or "turbulence", during which the singer may believe he will *never resolve* the antagonism between the two registers. Patience, faith, and persistence must reign!

Gradually, the "power factor" of the lower register will be permitted to pass beyond the registers break's, between E♮ and F♮ above middle C, to the tones above the registers' break, *but with none of its negative characteristics*—such as weight and/or thickness. As a result, the vibrato action of vocal cords, traveling on a concentrated stream of breath, enter into the top register's *resonance chambers*, and produce such amazing tonal qualities as: "ring", "resonance" and "projecting power", thereby adding all these, positive, formerly missing elements to the "thinner" *(although not weaker) top* tones of the developed upper register.

In this metamorphosed state, the two vocal registers, formerly antagonistic toward each other, finally start to "collaborate" in all tone production. This is often called a state of "coordinated registers". Now the singer can "thread" the power factor of the lower register into each and every tone of the upper register, along the ascending resonance channel, up to the topmost tones of his range.

While this process of reducing the bulk and weight of the lower register is occurring, a related phenomenon occurs with all the tones of the upper register. They begin to increase in number and can be extended beyond their borders at both ends, top and bottom, and begin to dominate a larger percentage of the complete vocal range.

When this advanced state of development is reached, the muscular action of the transformed upper register, which has been calculatingly brought downward to overlap the tones of the lower register, holds the "raw" action of the lower register "in check", so that it is forced to harmoniously join the muscular controls of the upper register, as opposed to challenging them. As a team, they produce beautiful, controllable vocal tones. This process of overlapping the tones of the lower register with the muscular controls of the upper register downward to the very bottom of the range is highly relevant to correct vocal structuring, and consistently produces extraordinary results. This difficult, time-consuming procedure represents one of the first major steps in the transference of the "dominance factor" of muscular control away from the lower register, and over to the upper register. *But the process must never deny the lower register to make its muscular contributions to all tone production.*

With continued strengthening of all the tones of the upper register, the basic sound of its tones begins to change. New, improved vocal sounds appear and begin to match the sounds of the transformed tones of the lower register. The lower register's tones begin to sound "lighter", "buoyant," and heady"; in time, they become *"puffy" (with breath),* and *"falsetto-like",* because the breath flow is now merging with them. They communicate to the singer *(and to the knowledgeable teacher),* their capacity to correctly apply "projecting power" as opposed to "forced resonance." At the same time, all the developing tones of the upper register begin to take on a more solid sound that is "like" the transformed sounds of the lower register, yet they are still being produced and controlled by the muscles of the upper register.

All these changes are to be expected and they are natural, when structuring procedures gives the upper register preferred treatment and development, with the intention of making the upper register's muscular controls dominate the entire vocal range.

All these altered *mixed sounds* are the result of the developing upper register and they precede the arrival of the *mezzo-falso (or "mixed voice" p. 79),* a mechanism of muscular control that results when the registers begin to approach muscular harmony with each other. Singers and teachers of the *Bel Canto* period *(about 1800),* termed these sounds the voce *di finta,* or *"feigned-voice".* The *mezzo-falso,* a modern version of the earlier term *voce di finta,* suggests that this mechanism, an outgrowth of the combined muscular actions of both registers, is capable of feigning or "pretending to be like" the original timbres *(and muscular actions)* of either, or both registers, on any given tone of the singer's complete vocal range. *Note that henceforth we will refer to the mezzo-falso as the mixed voice.*)

"Fiato Ferma"— the breath, ,irmly detained within the lungs

When this *mixed voice* mechanism appears, it allows the singer to initiate a soft falsetto tone in the upper register's domain, which to the listener sounds like a *detached* falsetto-sound, but which is actually the *mixed voice,* mechanism, which is capable of binding both registers to each other. The *mixed voice* allows the singer to press together *(by applying an intensified stream of breath pressure),* a combination of both registers' muscular actions, to accomplish the accuracy and prolongation of and selected pitch. When the two registers are tightly *"clamped"* together in this manner, the singer can add to any *mixed voice* tone the "bright, pulsing diamond-like" quality of the lower register, and also withdraw it, at will. This "clamping technique" was called *fiato-ferma,* by the great Italian teachers of the past; *fiato*—"breath held firmly and steadily in place", *ferma (short for fermare)*—"and held fast, still, and detained".

With some voices, this skill takes years to acquire.

Perhaps *Zinka Milanov,* the great Yugoslavian dramatic soprano, who studied with *Milka Ternina, (another great soprano from the past),* possessed the greatest and most beautiful *mixed voice* ever heard. *Miguel Fleta,* a Spanish tenor of the past, admired by Puccini, also possessed a marvelous sounding mixed voice. It has been reported that, *Montserrat Caballè,* upon hearing *Fleta's* recordings was so inspired that she became determined to develop a beautiful *mixed voce* of her own, which, indeed, she certainly did.

The cultivation of the *mixed voice* mechanism is a worthy goal for all singers to strive toward. It must operate throughout the entire range, so that the singer may easily pass back and forth from one register's muscular control to the other's, subjugating both registers to a "team effort". Presently, the *mixed voice* may only be heard with the voices of superior sopranos, even then, with limitations. But it is seldom heard with present-day, male singers, except for the lightest of tenor voices. But *Giuseppe Di Stefano,* a great tenor with a full-bodied voice, possessed a ravishing *mixed voice.*

Upon accomplishing this *mixed voice* control it advantageously nullifies the antagonism which inherently exists between registers. The term *voix mixte,* or "mixed voice" is a French term that was adapted from the Italian term *voce di finta.* However, "mixed voice", is inappropriately used because "mixed" implies that the separateness of the two registers could be transformed into a new and separate *single unit,* thereby becoming something totally different—like mixing salt and pepper together would produce a new black-and-white-speckled form of the two original elements. In reality, this is *not* what actually takes place. With the *mixed voice* appears, the muscular actions of each individual register never merge into a new, single unit. They remain separate entities, but function together as a "team". Their individual muscular actions lineup "side-by-side" while functioning together, in a vertical position, for the production of superior tone, while retaining their inherent individuality, as separate entities *(pgs. 98 & 99).*

While attempting to join both registers together on a selected tone, at a certain point in the swelling process, when and where the two registers first make contact with each other, there comes to exist a neutral response of both registers, to each other, which has been created by perfecting of the *messa di voce (p. 63).* The *messa di voce or* "swelled-tone", is accomplished by establishing a soft tone *(totally lacking in chest voice connection),* with the "detached falsetto" mechanism, then slowly increasing its volume until the full power of the chest voice is added to it. This can only be accomplished when the inherent power and bulk of the chest voice has been restructured, and the strength of the inherently weak falsetto voice has been brought to its maximum strength. This creates a neutral point of contact between both registers wherein neither one's power dominates the other's. Or, said another way, a point where the negative and uncooperative aspects of both registers have been neutralized.

In this state, the singer can "pinch" or "clamp" (*fiato ferma),* the muscles of both registers together, in the upper posterior area of the throat, and remain momentarily poised, ready to instigate the vocal need of the moment, whether to perform a *fortissimo* or *piano* tone, then fully launch the tone. The *mixed voice* mechanism grants the singer selectivity over the full range of dynamics, from soft to loud, and back to soft again, without either register's muscular controls challenging the muscular controls of the other register, nor the need for the singer to abandon the muscular controls of either register.

It is only when both registers' volume is suspended at this *desired neutral point* of soft, yet dynamic potential collaboration, that the singer can begin to execute a true *pianissimo.* The true *pianissimo* should display the timbres of *both* registers, but with the dynamic level of the chest register reduced to its minimum. A *"faked"* pianissimo tone utilizes the upper register exclusively *(without chest voice participation),* which results in a "wooly" tone without core substance. This kind of "vocal forgery" is in common usage by many professional singers today, and if used excessively it will eventually divide, then gradually erode the singer's complete vocal range, especially in the area of the registers' break.

The basic tools used for vocal exercises

In order for the singer to properly develop the muscles of the singing instrument, it is necessary for those muscles to be stressed. This is done by performing a series of exercises which progressively increase the amount of *breath pressure* tension being applied to them, until the desired developmental results is achieved. The process is not unlike progressive weight training. The tools that permit the application of *this desired stress* to the vocal muscles are:
1. Complete knowledge of what the breath tension of the *motor force* actual is, and how it should be applied.
2. Variations of amount breath tension, applied to a selected tone (s).
3. The application of the five classic Italian singing vowels, as pronounced by a native Italians.

1. Breath tension
(motor force)

The first basic tool for strengthening all underdeveloped tones is the application of *breath tension.* This is accomplished by inhaling air, then compressing and holding it back within the lungs, then directing it, *in the form of an intensified breath stream,* against the vocal cords. There are two cycles in the breathing process:
1. Intake: inhalation
2. Output: exhalation.

Inhalation must be executed very slowly. The main muscle involved with inhalation is the diaphragm, along with the help of other secondary muscles, located below the singer's lowest ribs. The diaphragm is to be activated first, while the muscles *located above the lowest ribs* are to be kept as passive as possible. This is referred to as *"low breathing"* and it allows the fullest amount of air to be inspired into the lungs. Even so, the amount of air *(breath tension)* to be used by the singer varies, depending on the pitch and phrase being presently sung.

At the end of the *intake cycle* of breath, after the lungs have become completely filled with air, *that air must be retained within the lungs by the singer and not expelled.* It is this retention of the air within the lungs which creates "breath tension", which in turn generates the motor force for singing.

In order to utilize the breath pressure that has built up in the lungs as the motor force for singing, the singer must inspire a generous or exaggerated amount of air into his lungs, then retain it for a brief moment, then he gradually expires it. But while doing so, he *must not* allow the air to "gush" out of his lungs, all at once. He must *instead* direct the outgoing *air stream* toward the vocal cords. Once the breath passes through the *glottis,* the opening between the vocal cords, it enters into the lower windpipe in the form of a narrow, intense stream of compressed air, and travels upward, along the resonance channel. The singer must direct this intensified stream of air backward and upward, past the soft and hard palates, so that it will travel further upward to the resonating cavities. These resonating cavities are located at the upper posterior area of the mouth-pharynx cavity, then higher upward, in the nasal cavities, and higher still, the resonating cavities in the skull. The individual pitch, being sung at any given moment, determines which of these cavities the singer must utilize.

It is important for the singer to understand that he must *definitely not* focus the traveling, stream of air into his mouth cavity, then forward and out of the mouth, past the front teeth. Unfortunately, during ordinary speech, this is precisely the *incorrect path* which the breath takes, for the average English speaking individual. This happens, rather automatically because, there are many more diphthongs in the English language *than pure vowels*, disadvantageously preventing the air stream from making a proper entrance into the vocal tract or passageway, on its own accord, and then traveling to an appropriate resonance channel. The point to remember is that pure vowels facilitate a correct pathway for the breath stream, upward and backward, and into and along the resonance channel's vertical ascending path.

Nor should the airflow be stopped, once it has arrived in any of the resonating cavities, since it must be prolonged therein and mix with the vibrations of the vocal cords, in order to generate the motor force for the presently sung pitch.

Earlier, in the breathing process, when the air first reaches the vocal cords, they react to this stream of traveling, energized breath *(the continuation of which is regulated by the diaphragm and various other muscles of the breathing apparatus),* by elastically yielding to its energy, in a series of rapid openings and closings. As the vocal cords yield to the stream of breath pressure being exerted against them, it causes a slight rise and fall in the pitch. This response is known as *vibrato*, and it *is a correct vocal action*, and is essential for correct singing.

Reacting in conjunction with, and in response to the application of the breath stream against the vocal cords, the *upper register's muscles pull upward,* while *the lower register's muscles pull downward.* Both registers, acting as a "team", in a "draw-string" manner, exert a counter-resistance to the energy to the breath tension that is being directed at the vocal cords. The vocal cords *vibrato action*, and the successful co-participation of the upper and lower registers upward-and-downward-pulls, depend completely upon a correct application of breath tension to these various muscular controls.

The singing tone is *not* produced by allowing the air to *gush* out of the lungs. One of the most misleading principles frequently told to students is: "Don't force the tone, let it float, effortlessly, on the breath." This implies that the singer is free from any "work load" in producing basic tone. *The superior tone is never free from any work load* because it is produced and prolonged by the *energy* of *compressed breath*, being retained by the singer within his lungs, and skillfully "fed" to the vocal cords, and which must flow continuously, for as long as he desires the presently sung tone to continue. As the singing voice mounts the scale to higher and higher pitches, the amount of breath pressure against the vocal cords must increase proportionately. And, an equally increased amount of *counter resistance*, created by the breath is applied by the muscles of both registers.

When the singer ascends the range, all of these factors make great demands upon him for *increased energy*. This is quite the opposite reality, from the wrong principle of "effortlessly produced singing". Conversely, when the singer descends the range from a higher pitch to a lower one, *the energy demand is reduced*, proportionately, as well as breath energy, *but the energy demand is never entirely eliminated.* There must always remain some amount of breath pressure being directed against the vocal cords, and breath continuously flowing through them, until the tone has been terminated. The continuous application of breath tension "holds" or "clamps" (*fiato ferma*), the two registers together, so that they serve as a counter-resisting force to the stream of breath pressure, flowing through the vocal cords, and producing the desired pitch.

Where singing is concerned, the least efficient way of breathing *is the shallow intercostal method*. Rather than the diaphragm being free *to expand downward and outward (as an expanding-and-contracting circle surrounding the waistline), it is incorrectly inverted upward*, and the entire chest cavity raised. This allows only a partial inhalation of breath and interferes with the attainment of a full breath, which is necessary to create the motor force for the production of tone. Singers who employ this incorrect *high breathing* method *(women, more frequently than men),* are incorrectly trying to *restrain* the collaboration of the chest voice. However, using correct *low breathing* will instead employ only the chest voice's *positive* contributions, *(this will be explained in detail, later.)* Singers using the incorrect, *high breathing method* tend to gulp for air, between phrases, raising their upper ribs and clavicles. This produces undesirable tensions with muscles that should remain passive, and it forbids thoracic expansion and the freedom of the diaphragm.

Correct breathing depends on coordinating the muscular *staying power of* exhalation. When breathing is correctly executed there is no deficiency of breath at the end of vocal phrases, but rather some excess, which must be expelled, before taking the next, new breath.

Admittedly, in order for the breathing system to grow progressively stronger the "breathing muscles" must be developed to their fullest. *However, they cannot be strengthened in a manner that is independent from the production of tone.* Their strengthening is conditioned upon, and regulated by the strengthening of the muscles of *both registers* while either singing or exercising the voice. As the muscular controls of the registers *(particularly the upper register),* grow in strength, so does the singer's capacity for correct and superior breathing.

To produce the wide range of vocal pitches contained in a given musical selection, *(low, middle, and top range),* varying amounts of compressed breath are required. *A lesser* or moderate amount of compressed breath is required for the *low and medium pitches*, and *a greater amount for the higher pitches*. While vocal tone is being sung, the vocal cords allow the breath, passing through the glottis, to escape in short, "puffy" blasts, while gradually and simultaneously dissipating the compressed breath, being restrained by the singer within his lungs. To maintain control of the duration of any given pitch, the singer must resist the rapid dissipation of breath tension, for the entire duration of the tone being sung.

Reacting from polarity positions *(from various throat positions, above and below the vocal cords),* both registers act together in *a drawstring manner*. As the breath pressure exerted against the vocal cords tends to move the entire vocal apparatus "forward", the counter-resistance of the two vocal registers tends to move it "backward". Despite the vocal apparatus' need for maintaining *mobility of movement* during the act of singing, these forces of the two registers, acting in unison, *maintain the proper position of the vocal apparatus*, relative to the production of tone being presently sung.

The growth of the breathing system's strength and effectiveness is conditional upon how long the singer can maintain the compressed air within his lungs, while producing a sustained, quality tone, and pure vowels. The longer the duration of a tone or phrase *(particularly with higher pitches),* the greater the stress which the breathing muscles must sustain. Therefore, the greater strengthening of the breathing muscles is accomplished, *when that stress can be successfully tolerated.* However, the muscles of the breathing system cannot accommodate these increases of stress unless the muscles of the two registers are developed to the point where they can produce equal amounts of counter-resistance.

2. *The three methods of applying breath tension dynamics to the singing instrument*

It is imperative that the singer develops the ability to apply varying amounts of breath tension to the muscles of the singing instrument. The breath tension, from the breath contained within the lungs, is the motor force for the singing voice. That force is applied through a variety of dynamic applications of breath tension, to various selected pitches. These breath applications permit the singer to apply the appropriate amounts of breath tension, according to the level of development of the muscles that produce a particular tone. The ability to progressively increase the necessary amount of breath tension can be developed through the utilization of a series of dynamic applications, varying from *minimum to maximum intensity*. These applications are the only way the singer has to adjust the softness or loudness of a tone (s). The tolerance for increased amounts of breath tension, while producing quality tone, determines the nature and pace of a muscle group's development. The figures below show the three options for applying dynamic variations of the breath stream, as outlined by the *Bel Canto School*:

Figure 1

The *messa di voce*

Figure 1 (above), the *messa di voce* : a tone is started *pp* and gradually swelled to *ff.*

Figure 2

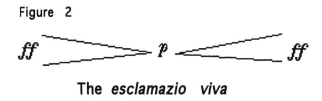

The *esclamazio viva*

Figure 2, the *esclamazio viva* : a tone is started with *ff* intensity, gradually reduced in volume to *p* intensity, then returned to its original intensity.

Figure 3

The *esclamazio languida*

Figure 3, the *esclamazio languida:* a tone is started with *p* intensity, gradually increased
To an *f* intensity, reduced again to *p intensity,* and finally increased to *ff* intensity.

The *messa di voce,* the *esclamazio viva,* and the *esclamazio languida* were the three most important exercises practiced during the *Bel Canto* era. For practical reasons, based on the needs of various voices, during critical stages of development, I have created a group of new exercises based upon these three classic exercises, which update their method of application to accommodate contemporary vocal repertory.

3. The five vocal vowels

To execute the various breath-dynamic-application-exercises necessary for developing the singing instrument, the singer must gain a complete understanding of the function of the five basic Italian vowels (oo), i (ee), e (eh), o (oh), and a (ah)—in their purest forms.

The Mechanical functions of the five singing vowels: u (oo), i (ee), e (eh), o (oh), and a (ah)

With every musical instrument, other than the singing voice, the performer can touch the instrument *directly with his hands* in order to exercise or play it. The singer's instrument, on the other hand, positioned as it is in his throat, and inaccessible, and can only be evoked and controlled *through the use of mental concepts and images* that critically relate to the function of the five basic vowels, which serve to set its physical mechanism in motion.

The vocal repertory involves a marriage of text and musical tones, and within any given word there is a dominating vowel that will correctly activate pure tone. Each vowel's functions must be clearly understood so that each may be utilized as a mentally-conceived "tool" or "control factor" permitting the singer reliable, accurate control of the singing instrument.

There is a *vast difference* between the technical requirements of the singing voice and those of the speaking voice. It is often *erroneously* suggested that the two function exactly alike. If this were so, the singer could easily sing any given word clearly, on any pitch, with the same ease and minimal energy as when speaking. It is *critically* important to distinguish between the *instrumental vowels* and the *spoken vowels*. As the singing voice rises in pitch, there is an unavoidable increase in volume, making it increasingly difficult for the singer to maintain pure vowels. Therefore, and to some degree, it is accepted that a compromise in "vowel purity" is inevitable in which the vowel's pronunciation is "modified". However, due to the lack of understanding of the vocal instrument's structural procedures and the critical part vowels play in constructing a superior vocal instrument, *"vowel modification"* has become *an excuse* for the lack of structural information about the singing vowels, and an excuse for blurring the vowels to a point extreme. The singer must learn how to structure the five "singing vowels" to their purest level, while still allowing for the physiological limitations of obtaining perfectly *"pronounced"* singing vowels throughout his complete range.

The chief focus of any vocal training program must be to establish a primary condition of upper register dominance throughout the voice's range, and it is critical that a preferred vowel be selected at the *onset* of this process. It is best vowel to start with the *u (oo) vowel*, as it represents the purest manifestation of the upper register, which is fundamental to the Head Voice/Falsetto system of training. In all exercises given, the Italian pronunciation of each vowel, *as spoken by native Italians*, must be used.

It should be noted that each of the five vowels responds differently when it is applied to the tones of the *chest voice*, than when each it is applied to the *head voice*. Henceforth, we shall refer to these different behavioral patterns as *chest voice mode* and *head voice mode*, respectfully.

I. The u (oo) vowel

The u (oo) vowel readily serves to both purify and identify the difference between the two registers. The purification process eliminates radical muscular conflicts within the tones of a purified register. The u (oo) vowel is the *"headiest"* of all the vowels—whereas a (ah) is the most *"chesty"* vowel. The u (oo) vowel permits a clear comparison of the two registers. This is due to the *polarity* in quality and muscular functions that exists between the two registers. The quality of the *undeveloped chest register* is "solid" and "resonant", and its muscular actions are "thick" and "weighty". The quality of the *undeveloped falsetto register's* quality is "soft" and "sweet" and often "breathy", and its muscular actions are "thin" and "light", and it produces many muted sounds.

When exercising the voice, the use of the u (oo) vowel permits the singer to readily distinguish all sound qualities and muscular actions of the head voice, from the qualities and muscular actions of the chest voice. In the case of the successfully-trained singing voice, neither register's function is ever denied, as they are permanently interdependent. More significantly, they are synergistic; the two registers, when coupled, make possible a voice that could not otherwise exist.

The u (oo) vowel can serve to *purify and repair* the other four vowels, during the long process of registers blending, and especially so at the beginning of training, when it is necessary to temporarily restrain the chest voice. In the *first phase* of voice structuring, the *closed phase*, whenever any of the four other vowels, other than the u (oo), becomes distorted and/or its action confusing, thereby causing vocal disruption, it is the u (oo) vowel which singer can restore the tone and its vowel to muscular purity and grant the singer a new start in developing it. Applying the u (oo) vowel to a selected pitch, accompanied by a full flow of the breath stream, nullifies any structural mistake (s) which has been applied to it. The purification process is not an "immediate" obtainment, and the length of time necessary to undo incorrectly muscular arrangements with the u (oo) vowel varies, and is relative to how much. and how long the abuse has been applied.

In the beginning, *closed phase* of voice structuring, starting with underdeveloped muscles, the u (oo) is excellent for understanding the correct, developmental sequence of vowels *(a smooth muscular adjustment when passing from one vowel to another),* accomplished in the following manner. The singer starts a tone with u (oo), then, with the same pitch, without taking a new breath, he slowly changes it *(without diminishing the breath tension),* to an i (ee) vowel, then to an e (eh) vowel, then to an o (oh) vowel, and finally to an a (ah) vowel. *This is the ideal, permanent order of the vowels* during the first, closed phase of training. Performing this sequence results in the maximum harmony of muscular response, which can be readily felt, while passing from one vowel to the next.

If any vowel is removed from this superior order and placed in another position amongst the other vowels, during the transition from one vowel to the next, muscular accuracy and harmony are temporarily denied, and disruptive muscular movements result which cause undesirable sounds. However, there comes a point of advanced muscular development when the singing voice progresses to an *"open phase".* At that point, this earlier ruling about the ideal, permanent order of the vowels is *changed from a closed to an open one.* The differences between "closed" and "open" phases of development will be explained later.

Admittedly, when the singer departs from vocal exercises and sings a musical piece, the ideal sequence of the vowels become "scrambled" out of order. Nevertheless, while exercising, to perfect the vowels, it is essential to maintain this specific order, as a standard of reference for each vowel's purity. When properly applied, the u (oo) vowel possesses an inherent ability to engage the purest and greatest percentage of upper register muscle action, and *deny* any undesirable chest voice, muscular participation.

Should a "breathy" quality appear when using the u (oo) vowel, the singer could easily misunderstand this to be a faulty action. Rather, it is a natural manifestation of the u (oo) vowel, The u (oo) vowel also allows the singer to monitor the breath flow accompanying the production of any selected tone. Whenever the singer produces a tone incorrectly, the breath flow, which generates the tone, stops flowing, denying the motor force that generates it. This undesirable *breath stoppage* is generally accompanied by a feeling of "throat-tightness" and lower jaw rigidity, and indicates that the singer has applied the wrong muscle (s) to the tone.

Another fact about the u (oo) vowel is that, more than any other vowel, it most resists strengthening throughout the vocal range, especially in the Registers' Break area, and at the lower area of the singer's range, where the lower register's power originates. The u (oo) *does not* reveal its total structural potentials until very late in the structuring process. During the earlier phase of training, the u (oo) vowel often *seems* to be a most improbable solution for correctly structuring the singing instrument.

One frequent misinterpretation of the u (oo) vowel applications is that they "smother the "brightness" of the voice. This is an early, erroneous impression. This wrongly perceived "smothering" of the voice's *bright quality,* is in reality, the u (oo) vowel's positive manner of *denying* the chest voice's negative actions. With continued use, even when not completely understanding the u (oo) vowel's beneficial influences completely, in time, applying the u (oo) vowel will prove to be one of the most effective of all vocal structuring tools.

With proper usage, the u (oo) permits the singer to subjugate the inherent muscular antagonism between the two registers, especially in the registers' break area, and also to reorder these two combative forces into a cooperative "team" effort. When vocal "graduation" draws near, the u (oo) vowel *(along with the o (oh) vowel),* serves to "round" and polish the voice to a professional level, because it alone can guide the accumulated buildup of "tonal power", produced by the advanced muscular development of the other four vowels, to a state of beauty, and advanced control. It is a tragic fact that, with most present-day teaching methods, the u (oo) vowel is the most misunderstood and least applied of all the five vowels.

II. The i (ee) vowel

With English speaking Americans, the i (ee) vowel's "head voice form" *(as opposed to its chest voice, "speaking voice" form),* is perhaps the most difficult of the five vowels for them to understand, access, and apply. The i (ee) vowel's head voice form is the only form that can be used to structure the singing voice. It's "chest voice" form may only be employed *after* it has been appropriately structured by its "head voice" form, through many applications of the messa *di voce exercises.* The detached falsetto, "head voice" form of the i (ee) vowel is permanently related to the u (oo) vowel, and like the u (oo) vowel, it encourages the flow of breath, while its chest voice form block the breath flow. When there is confusion about how to exercise or sing either the u (oo) or the i (ee) vowel, the singer should relate the one that is causing confusion to the other.

The *detached falsetto, head voice version of the* i (ee) vowel inherently and involuntarily pulls the tone upward in the opposite direction from the chest voice' downward pull, *and* focuses the presently sung tone toward the highest pitch of the singer's vocal range. But this *"upward pulling"* can only happen when the i (ee) vowel is operating in its purest, *head voice mode,* meaning when it is *"not anchored"* in any way, and it is being produced by a full, free flow of breath.

When the i (ee) is operating in its *chest voice mode* it stops the breath flow. Therefore, the chest voice mode of the i (ee) vowel can only be used when it is coupled to the advanced developed falsetto, i (ee), vowel. This automatic "upward-pointing positioning" of the open i (ee) vowel can be used advantageously to engage *only the desired muscular actions and qualities of the lower register*, especially when ascending the range. This important i (ee) vowel counteracts the lower register's tendency to pull the voice downward and make it "thick" and "weighty", which causes any selected tone to break away from proper registers' alignment, particularly while ascending the vocal tract.

At the start of training, when attempting to unite the two registers, the tones of the upper register strongly resist coupling with the tones of the lower register *(especially at the point in the complete vocal range where the registers meet each other, between En and Fn above middle C.* Both registers' resistance to being "connected" to each other oftentimes manifests itself with a *"snapping away from each other"* action. When this snapping apart occurs, the muscles of the i (ee) vowel zoom upward toward the top of the range. In a related manner, the tones of the lower register resist coupling with the Upper Register, by breaking away from the upper register and "falling downward".

For a tone to be superior, it must display beauty of sound, accuracy of pitch, and absolute control of all levels of breath intensity. To achieve a vowel's correct "throat positioning", on all ascending tones, the singer must aim the tone *upward* and *backward* in the mouth-pharynx cavity *(definitely not "forward" or "into the mask"),* and toward the highest pitch of the complete range. The "tuning" vowel i (ee), when functioning in its pure, falsetto mode—meaning that it is free from all negative chest voice weight and power—and "riding freely" on the breath flow, guides the singer in this accomplishment. Later on in this manual more details about the benefits of detached falsetto i (ee) vowel will be given which explains how it, and it alone, is capable of calibrating "the thinness/thickness factor," of any and all tones of the singer's complete range.

"The mask" is a vocal term that attempts to describe the "triangular" area of the face formed by the positions of the eyes, nose and mouth, behind which are located the *mouth-pharynx* and *sinus and head cavities*. Students are incorrectly instructed to "direct a selected tone into the mask", supported by the false belief that a superior tone can be created *solely and exclusively by, and* within "the mask" itself. What actually happens with a correctly sung tone when it is located between middle C and the Fn above it *(the range of "the mask"),* is that all the various factors of superior tone: a correctly produced vowel, the harmonious collaboration of both registers' muscular actions, and the precise application of the breath flow, allow the tone to *sympathetically resonate* within either the mouth-pharynx cavity, or within the nasal, and/or head cavities, the same anatomical regions of the so-called "mask". This "mask" theory can mistakenly lead the singer-student to believe that the tone (s) is generated inside the "mask" area. That *is not possible*, since these resonance cavities are *not* capable of generating the *vibrato action* of the vocal cords, a necessary factor for creating a superior tone, which can only be accomplished by the vocal cords, and thereafter, its appropriate resonance cavity r̲esonates, amplifies, and enhances the pulsing sounds of the vibrato action of the tone, within the selected resonance chamber, which has first been generated by the vocal cords, located far below these resonance cavities.

The difference between attempting to create a selected tone within "the mask", and directing the breath stream, transporting the tone upward, along the resonance tract, behind the soft and hard palates and into the proper resonating cavity, is that the singer comes to understand the nature of the motor force of the breath, and also how to direct it to its precise terminal "hookup" point, located within any of the various resonance cavities.

These individual *"hookup points"* are located at specific places along the posterior lining of mouth-pharynx and head cavities. The singer starts a tone by energizing the vocal cords with the breath flow, which passed through the glottis, after which, the singer must direct it upward and backward toward the posterior part of the throat, behind the soft and hard palates, and into one of the resonance cavities.

The production of all correct, superior tones requires a dual-phase operation: *Phase l*, the generation of the tone by the vocal cords, and *Phase 2, the act of directing the tone, traveling on the breath flow, backward and upward toward its corresponding "hookup point", and into either the mouth-pharynx, or head/sinus cavities*. Once that's accomplished, the selected tone connects with its appropriate terminal *"hook up point"* of impingement. These "hookup" points" will be discussed in detail later *(pg. 75)*.

When executing an ascending scale or vocal phrase, placing an open i (ee) vowel *(when in its correct detached falsetto mode and bases upon the open position of the a (ah) vowel),* in front of any of the other three vowels, the e (eh) o (oh) and a (ah), provides the singer with an infallible "pointer/tuner" vowel. This *pointer/tuner vowel* guides the other vowels correctly upward and backward in the throat along the pathway of the ascending vocal scale. The end result of this achievement is traditionally termed "correct vocal placement".

One hazard of the i (ee) vowel is that it may lead the singer to incorrectly select its "chest voice mode", and focus the tone too far "forward" and into the mouth cavity. When correctly sung the i (ee) should bypass the front of mouth cavity and ascend the *posterior pathway* at the upper, rear area of the throat, pass behind the soft palate, which responds by moving downward and forward, to clear a passageway for the breath to pass freely by, then further up in the range, through *passaggio*, whose throat-spaces are the narrowest and smallest of all the tones of the tenor's complete range of tones, then further upward to the top range.

If the i (ee) vowel is *incorrectly* "placed", it "hooks" into the thick muscles of the chest voice and stops the tone completely, or forces it to break away from "head voice" collaboration, and deny *legato* passage from one vowel to another. This causes registers' imbalances throughout the vocal range, resulting in disruptive muscular responses between the various sections of the vocal tract. The "runaway" i (ee) vowel must be constantly checked, by starting with an open a (ah) vowel, then passing the i (ee) vowel through the a (ah) vowel's *throat position*, without taking a new breath. This will help the singer understand the correct throat position and focus of the i (ee) and guide it along its correct singing pathway, upward behind the soft palate. This process will return the faulty i (ee) vowel to its correct harmonious relationship with the remaining four vowels, and away from the *incorrect* "forward" position in the mouth cavity, and toward the front teeth.

The i (ee) vowel can be most effectively used when executing ascending scales, to establish the correct singing pathway for the other vowels. Particularly when a scale ascends from Fn above middle C, and to the higher notes above it. This open i (ee) vowel will "thin down" all the tones of a rising vocal scale, in a positive manner, and help it avoid dragging the thick, muscular mass of the chest register upward, an into what I term the "wide registers' break area", specifically, from Bf below middle C to the Fn above it. It will also teach the singer, by nature of its thinness, which does not in any way deny the singer the fullest intensity of the breath flow, how to "switch" the muscular controls of any tone away from the chest voice's muscular controls, and over to the head voice's muscular controls.

The correctly produced i (ee) vowel is also helpful for discovering the much-desired *mixed voice*, which is an advanced mechanism of vocal control derived from the advanced development of the falsetto muscles.

III. The e (eh) vowel

The e (eh) vowel is neither a *"closed"* nor an *"open"* vowel, as it does not specifically favor the muscular actions of either the lower register or the upper register. It inherently brings into play approximately *fifty percent* of each registers' muscular influences, thus making it the *"midway"* vowel, in the process of singing through the "ideal passage of the five vowels", staring with an u (oo) passing to the i (ee), arriving at the e (eh) vowel *(at the "midway point")*, then proceeding to the o (oh) vowel, the first *open* vowel, then finally arriving at the a (ah) vowel, *the most open-throated vowel of all*, and the most difficult to master. The e (eh) allows the singer to guide the throat-position of any given tone from a closed throat position toward a "more open" throat position, as when singing the a (ah) vowel. The terms "closed" and "open" throat positions refer to the various positions of the posterior area of the throat, and frontally, the position which the lips must assume, when each individual vowel is purely formed in the throat.

With each of the five classic Italian vowels, the singer is unavoidably obliged to adjust the throat and lips positions, according to the particular vowel being presently sung. *An ideal throat position is relevant to the purest standard of the vowel being presently sung.* The various positions of the throat and the lips range from a *fully closed position*, while singing the u (oo) and the i (ee) "closed" vowels, *to a fully opened position of the throat and lips* when singing the a (ah) vowel. These positions of the vowel's throat sockets, imposed by each individual vowel, take priority over the positing of the lips, which are secondary.

As a visual aid, the singer may stand before a mirror and sing a comfortable pitch using the open o (oh) vowel, generated by a free flow of breath, then changing it to the "midway" open e (eh) vowel, noting in the mirror the shifting lips' positions, when passing from the o (oh) vowel to the e (eh) vowel.

As to all the various positions of the posterior area of the throat, where each of the five vowels is concerned, they are learned gradually, with the progressive development of the two registers, since only with the registers fullest development can the appropriate throat position be accomplished and revealed, for each individual vowel.

While the e (eh) vowel incorporates equal proportions of the muscular actions of the upper and lower registers, it also allows the singer to select various percentages of the two registers' timbres and muscular actions. The e (eh) vowel can be compared to a fulcrum point. When a tone seems too "thick" and "weighty" the singer may adjust the e (eh) vowel's throat position by adding more i (ee) vowel influence to the tone. Conversely, when he feels the tone is too "thin" and "brittle", he may direct the e (eh) vowel more toward the muscular influences of the "wider" o (oh) vowel or in some cases toward the a (ah) vowel's throat socket.

The e (eh) vowel is often favored by large-voice singers because, more than any of the other vowels, as it keeps the voice's muscular actions from too much thinning or thickening. The (eh) vowel most readily allows the large-voice singer a choice of "register proportioning", according to the vocal need of the moment. When the singer has structured his voice to its fullest development, *all correct* lips and throat positions are more readily available to him, than they are to a singer with underdeveloped registers. Therefore, advanced singers are capable of producing purer vowels than can singers with *underdeveloped registers*. Furthermore, while an advanced singer is singing a particular vowel, the purest throat and lips positions of the four remaining vowels, although not active at the moment, are readily available, and allows the singer either a slow or rapid change of vowels.

IV. The o (oh) vowel

The o (oh) vowel, when operating in its *chest voice mode*, greatly favors the muscular actions and qualities of the chest voice. However, *in its head voice mode*, the o (oo) has a great affinity with the u (oo) vowel. Should there be any confusion regarding the o (oo) vowel's exact pronunciation and register proportions, this can be clarified by utilizing the o (oh) vowel's own *tuning* vowel, the u (oo), in its early, *closed, head voice phase* of development. This may be accomplished by starting with the u (oo) vowel, then passing on to an o (oh) vowel, then returning to the starter u (oo) vowel's throat position, then taking note of the relationship between the u (oo) and o (oh) vowel. Later on, when the muscles of the upper register reach the *open phase* of development, the o (oh) vowel must frequently, although not always, be made to relate to the open a (ah) vowel.

But during the earlier *"closed phase"* of training, in order to establish the precise pronunciation of the o (oh) vowel, the singer should selected a tone with an u (oo) vowel then gradually change it to the o (oh) vowel, then return to the u (oo) vowel, all on the same pitch and without taking a new breath. In the beginning of training, North Americans tend to permit the pronunciation of the o (oh) vowel to immediately and consistently relate to the a (ah) vowel, and this is *incorrect*, since the o (oh) vowel should relate to the u (oo) vowel for quite some time before the singer may relate it to the a (ah) vowel's more open throat position.

As the voice develops, the o (oh) vowel may also be utilized to *"preset"* muscular conditions in the throat to achieve the correct throat positioning of the a (ah) vowel, especially with the tenors lower notes, below middle C. This *"presetting"* technique is essential, since, the a (ah) vowel is the most difficult of the five vowels to perfect with the tenor's lowest tones. Of course, many students will doubt that fact, since they can easily evoke the *incorrect* a (ah) vowel, which grants them ample volume, and deceives them into thinking they are correct a (ah) vowel tones. However, the student will quickly learn that these incorrect lower tone a (ah) vowels will destroy his passaggio completely and deny him access to his top most tone.

This is so *because* the incorrect a (ah) vowel *involuntarily pulls into play the negative actions of*

Anthony Frisell—28

the lower register and it resists *"connection"* and proper coordination with the protective actions of the *mixed voice*, which grants the singer the only possible method of dynamic control over the a (ah) vowel. By utilizing the o (oh) vowel to guide the a (ah) into its proper throat position, the difficult a (ah) vowel may be carefully and exactly placed into its correct throat space and joined to the head voice muscles.

One of the most significant ways in which the o (oh) vowel differs from the a (ah) vowel is that the *undeveloped o (oh) vowel* tends to have a "muted" and "hollow" texture, which is appropriate. The singer may try to compensate for this "hollowness" by reaching toward the a (ah) vowel of the chest voice, in an attempt to add core brilliance and "stabilization" to the tone, which seems to be missing. The singer *must not* do this. Instead, he must patiently allow the o (oh) vowel to retain its "muted", "hollow" and "unstable" behavior, until the upper register has been cultivated to an advanced state wherein the *mixed voice* mechanism appears. This mixed voice mechanism grants the singer the proper way to add "core" brilliance to the o (oh) vowel. He should wait until an almost perfect set of o (oh) tones and scales have been mastered before proceeding to the more difficult open a (ah) vowel. The advanced open o (oh) vowel grants the singer a "well rounded voice" that possesses such admired qualities as "smoothness", "velvety rich", "floating" tones that are associated with superior singers, and which give his listeners the impression that his singing is "effortless".

V. The a (ah) vowel

The a (ah) favors the muscular actions of the *chest register* more than any of the other vowels. In many cases, it favors the lower register *excessively,* so that it *excludes* the important muscular actions and timbres of the upper register, thereby denying the significant benefits of the u (oo) and the i (ee) vowels, which are indispensable aids for preventing the potentially negative activities of the lower register from destroying the correct functions, beauty, and *posterior throat pathway* of all ascending scales and phrases.

The a (ah) vowel is the one that most quickly deceives the novice into believing that strong, superior tones have been quickly achieved. However, they are often incorrect "chesty" tones that *will not* let him sing through the registers' break area. Generally, these incorrectly structured a (ah) vowels result from using the harmful "Chest Voice" method of voice production, a system of training which so many teachers of today practice, which involves the application of many ascending scales, with the "wide open" damaging a (ah) vowel, plus the damaging principle of voice training which *related all* tones to the same muscles as the speaking voice.

In the Fourth Century, the revered *Scuola Cantorum, a musical conservatory established by Pope Sylvester to instruct members of the clergy and the choir on the principles of vocal production and musical theory,* concluded, after much time and careful investigation, *that a singer should be warned against the a (ah) vowel and its potential for forcing the lower portion of the vocal range upward past the point of the registers' break, without bringing in the requisite amount of falsetto or upper register activity to aid in the addition of tonal solidity.* Essentially, this concept has remained entirely valid until present times.

When a brilliant "Italianate" a (ah) vowel is correctly produced, *its negative potentials has been negated by the singer "rounding it off" toward the open o (oh) vowel,* and his always making sure that the "rounded" a (ah) vowel is accompanied by a free flow of the breath stream. The "rounded" a (ah) vowel's sound, especially with the voices of advanced singers, can deceive the listener into believing that it has a great deal of lower register action in it. The opposite is true—*the correct a (ah) possesses more upper register domination.*

If the singer believes that he has achieved a near-perfect a (ah) vowel, it can be tested by first establishing a selected tone with *his* "near perfect" a (ah) vowel, noting its quality and throat position, then terminating it. Then he should establish a new tone with the o (oh) vowel, then slowly change it to a "rounded" a (ah) vowel. If his first a (ah) vowel, the one considered to be "near perfect", matches the high standards of the second, new a (ah) vowel, which was accomplished by passing it through from the "rounding off", open o (oo) vowel, *only then* can he say that a near-perfect a (ah) vowel has been achieved.

The five basic vowels, in their various "pronunciation forms" and "throat positions", are capable of considerable *modification*, so that the muscular activities and vocal timbers of one vowel may be merged with any other. While this adds a rich variety of tonal colors to the singer's vocal palette, these modifications are deviations from the vowels' *ideal, pure form*. As such, *the modification process could easily degenerate all the vowels from their pure form*. It is therefore imperative that the purity of each vowel be periodically reviewed. The above section of this manual, concerning the five "classic Italian vowels", is merely a *brief sketch* of what all the vowels are capable of contributing to the singer's achieving success with this training program. As the manual unfolds, many more technical factors about the five classic, Italian vowels will be presented.

Locating the "Registers' Break"

Tenors may locate the position of their *"Registers' Break"* by executing an eight-tone scale, in an ascending direction. Start the scale with A♭ below middle C, with medium volume, and an a (ah) vowel, and slowly ascend the scale to the A♭, an octave above.

Individuals tend to argue over the actual location of the registers' break *from their personal point of view*, claiming to be right about its location, while believing that others are *"dead"* wrong. What causes these vast differences of opinions is the fact that the behavior of the muscles of either or both registers, in the critical "break area", can *be altered*. If this were not a so, it would *not* be *possible* to resolve the problems of the registers' break area, at all.

Those tenors who can produce the suggested ascending scale (below), as if all its tones were *a single muscular unit*, making only minor, mechanical adjustments, but still producing a resonant, superior tone quality, have *solved the problems of the "registers' break,* to some degree. However, this is a most *uncommon vocal state*. Generally most beginning tenors possess *divided, dysfunctional registers* which forces them to make *a major mechanical adjustment* in the "break area", in order to complete an ascending scale with a good "resonant" quality and pure vowels. In many cases the singer is unable to complete the scale.

Area of mandatory adjustment in the tenor range when encountering the registers' break.

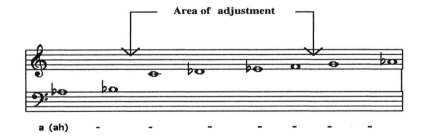

The illustration above presents an ascending scale for locating the position of the Registers' Break. The a (ah) vowel should be used, since it is the most challenging and revelatory. One of two more scales may be tried, raising the scale a half tone, then lowering it a half tone. The registers' break *(or "dividing-point"),* is located between E♮ and F♮, above middle C—*see p. 6.* While proceeding upward with the scale, and before reaching the top A♭, the singer will have to make either a major mechanical adjustment, by transferring the basic method of tones production away from the lower register's muscular controls and over to the upper register's muscular controls, or *fail* to complete the scale without *"forcing"* and producing inferior sounds. This adjustment may occur anywhere between middle C and the Fn above it,

The Tenor's Vocal Range

A strong point must be made here, about the way the tenor's vocal range is written in most currently printed vocal scores. Although the tenor's complete range of vocal tones is *presently* written *entirely within the treble clef staff,* in actuality, the tenor's complete range of tones *straddles the treble and bass clefs (see the illustration below).*

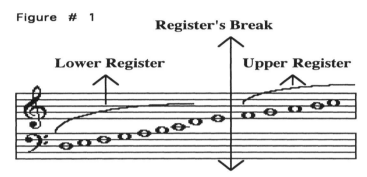

Figure # 1

Register's Break

Lower Register   **Upper Register**

Actual location of the tenor's range of vocal tones, "straddling" both bass and treble clefs.

The illustration above shows the *actual location* of the tenor's vocal range of tones ,and his registers' break, located between E♮ and F♮ above middle C. Review the *illustrations above to the right,* which shows the *old, discarded clef symbol* for the tenor voice. At some point in past, printing history, it was decided that it would be more convenient to transcribe the tenor's complete range of tones an octave upward, and completely into the treble clef. However, in terms of vocal training, this was a mistake. Presently, the tenor, reading his music from the printed page, *hears all the tones of his complete range as being an octave above their actual pitches, as written in the score before him.*

The old, discarded clef symbol for the Tenor Voice

It is common practice to use the piano, as a training instrument, to give the singer his starting pitch, to guide him in singing exercise scales, songs, or operatic roles. When the starting pitch is given an *octave higher* than the singer actually sings it, *(due to historical ignorance),* the *discrepancy between the actual vibrations per second of the note sounded on the piano,* and the actual ones that he must sing, using his vocal organs, consistently denies the tenor a realistic sense of harmony and accuracy. It is then advisable for tenors, voice teachers, and coaches, working with tenors, to play the tenor's starting pitch for him, in the actual octave in which it is located, *an octave lower than where it is presently written on the printed page.*

At most, the well developed, *superior tenor voice* functions best within a range of fourteen whole notes from F♮ below middle C, to the B♭ above middle C. And with a *tenor of average development,* between B♭, below middle C, to the B♭ Above middle C. This means that within that small range, the tenor produces his most consistent, effective, functional, quality tones. Thus, the tenor has a relatively short range, when compared to female voices. This is because, in order for the tenor to maintain the proper proportions of both head voice and chest voice, from middle C to the B♭ above it, he must use very few "chest tones" below middle C. Even though many vocal compositions are scored to include high C's and D's, in the upper range, and low tones, below F♮ below middle C, in reality, the tenor's most comfortable range of singing is from F♮ below middle C to the B♭ above middle C. Those who can negotiate the extremes of high C and above, plus some of the lower tones of E♮, E♭, D♮ *below* middle C, possess exceptionally well developed voices, with completely collaborative vocal registers, and they use them skillfully. They are the exception, however.

There have been many legendary stories, passed down through the past years, describing the extreme range of certain tenors of the early *bel canto* era, praising their great feats of vocal agility, flexibility, and soaring "high notes". The earlier works of *Rossini, Bellini, and Donizetti,* which these legendary tenors sang, abound in high notes, with a great deal of *fioritura* singing *("flowery, fast moving, vocal ornamentations"),* however, the technical manner of singing upper tones *then* was much *different than what we presently hear* in our concert halls and opera houses. In the past, there was more "falsetto quality" to all their upper tones than *"chest voice"* quality. Historically, *Gilbert-Louis Duprez (1806-1896),* is reported to have been the first tenor *"to successfully transport the full power of his chest register above the registers' break, to high C."*

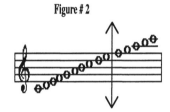

Figure # 2

The frequently mistaken concept of where the Tenor's registers' break is located

The illustration to the right shows *the often mistaken concept* of where *the tenor's registers' break* is located, between E♮ and F♮ above middle-C2, toward the top of the soprano's range. If this were true, it would place all the tones of the tenor's range within the borders of the treble staff. However, this is not accurate, since the tenor's complete range of tones *"straddle" the bass and treble clefs (see the illustration to the previous page).*

Like tenor *Gilbert-Louis Duprez,* present-day tenors are expected to sing their upper tones with a great amount of *"chest resonance",* drawn from the lower register, which limits both their upper extension and vocal flexibility. If our present-day tenors were to sing their upper tones in a "falsetto manner", as was done in the past, before the event of *Duprez's* famous *"do di petto"* their falsetto-production of their upper tops notes would be criticized as being "false" and unrelated to the rest of their "natural, male voice".

Since the advent of the *verismo* school of vocal composition, singers are required to produce more vocal volume, to cope with the fuller orchestrations of *Verdi, Berlioz, Puccini, Bizet, Gounod, Jules Massenet,* and other composers of this school, plus the heroic operas of *Richard Wagner,* who placed the accent of their compositions upon "the drama"; quite contrary to the sentiments of the *florid style* of early *Donizetti, Bellini, and Rossini,* and others such as *Pergolesi,* and *Cimarosa,* who placed more importance on the beauty and purity of the voice, and the evenness and smoothness of its *"vocal line".* A study of the phonograph recordings of a few past great tenors, *Caruso, Tamagno, Pertile, Lauri-Volpi, Zanatello, DeLucia, Gigli, Schipa and Bonci,* and some more recent tenors, *Bjöerling, Vinay, Del Monico, Corelli, Tucker, Di Stefano* reveals that generally, their most comfortable, "quality singing range" doesn't extend much beyond B♮, above middle C, and low D♮ below middle C. This is not to find fault with these artists. All deserve the title *great.* It is merely stated as a technical observation.

Never force the Lower Register upward

Most present-day methods of teaching singing unintentionally use damaging vocal exercises which force the lower register upward toward the registers' break. These exercises generally consist of a series of rote, meaningless ascending scales which slur over the important, highly detailed structuring procedures of superior training, which require specific knowledge and careful applications. This upward forcing of the voice is both damaging and highly unmusical, and does not permit the singer to extend his range any further than the E♮ above middle C. When the range will not be extended by "forced resonance", other methods are tried, such as reducing the volume, exercising solely with one vowel *(usually the incorrect, thick chest voice mode of the voice i (ee) vowel)*, and/or "*covering*", a method of holding back the intensity and "brightness" of the chest voice from the tone, resulting in a "blurred" "wooly" sound.

None of these methods work, and after repeated failures have proven that the lower register cannot be extended beyond E♮ above middle C, the solution to the problem can be found by developing the falsetto's range of tones. At first this is very confusing to the singer. The *falsetto must be brought downward to overlap the entire lower register. Only then will it be possible to extend the singer's range upward, beyond E♮ above middle C, correctly and musically!*

Tenors, of all vocal categories, *can least tolerate* these present-day, "overly chesty" ascending scales, usually assigned to them. The tenor voice develops from, and finds it best method of being structured, by applying special exercises to the pitches of the register's break, E♭, E♮, F♮, and F♯ above middle C.

The most essential element for extending the tenor's range above the *passaggio,* to all the tones above it, is to exercise the *head voice's muscles* until they become transformed into the *mezzo-falso,* or *mixed voice (to be explained later.)*

The use of this *"head voice"* training method, as presented in this manual, has long since disappeared from vocal studios of the world. Perhaps it was first lost or deliberately denied when the falsetto itself, was no longer considered useful in training the male singing voice. (See the article at the end of this manual—*"Is there an American School of Voice training? And if so, has it failed American Singers?"*

Tenors can hear actual examples of the ways in which the *mixed voiced* is skillfully employed in tone production by listening to phonograph recordings of *Gigli, Schipa, Miguel Fleta, John McCormack, Jan Kiepura, Nicolai Gedda, Joseph Schmidt,* and the young *Giuseppe DiStefano.*

Some tenors can quickly accumulate a limited range of inferior tones which are negatively dominated by the chest voice muscles, and which *limit* the muscular controls of the head voice, denying their vocal progress. These tenors lack control of all the softer dynamics and can only sing loudly. They usually excuse their vocal limitation by labeling themselves *"dramatic tenors",* as if being a *"dramatic tenor"* allowed them to dispense with all vocal finesse.

Since all the tones of the tenor's vocal range *must* be dominated by the head voice's muscular controls, after they have been corrected been structured, the serious student, must seek out and eliminate those *"raw chest tones"* at the bottom of his range, which still remain outside the *broad arc* of the head voice's complete dominance, and devote his full attention to cultivating the small "falsetto sounds", with all of them. As these "small" but appropriate, falsetto top tones seem, , at the beginning of developing them, unrelated to the *"normal", "manly"* qualities associated with the performing voice, most student-tenors will pay little attention to this sound advice. However, unless these seemingly "unimportant falsetto sounds" *are* cultivated to their fullest muscular potential, the singer is inviting a short-lived period of seemingly rapid vocal development *followed by complete vocal failure.*

CHAPTER THREE

"Breath Support"

Throughout this manual the word *intensity* will be frequently used to indicate the loudness or softness of a given vocal tone. The physiological factors necessary for producing these intensity controls are related to the ways in which the singer uses the "breath stream" to create a *motor force* that activates a given pitch. The part played by the breathing apparatus in vocal tone production has been wrongly characterized to such a degree that it has contributed more confusion than good. The student's breathing method is often blamed, when vocal faults persist and the teacher lacks the technical know-how to correct them. Almost any layman can quote such typical vocal-training phrases as, *"sing from the diaphragm"*, *"support the voice from below"*, or the most confusing, *"produce the tone with the diaphragm"*. All contain a certain relevance, however one would assume from them that the voice is produced solely by the breathing apparatus itself, *without* the participation of the other vocal organs.

In the beginning of vocal training, the limited development of the muscles of the vocal registers *will not* permit the student to use the complete range of dynamics of his breath power. An example of the interdependency between correct breathing and the development of the muscles of the registers can be understood when certain professional singers, after a long period of successful singing, show obvious difficulty in sustaining long vocal phrases. *Surely they have not forgotten how to breathe?* Logically then, the problem must be attributed to other factors. Frequently, the cause is some irregular function of the vocal registers which do not allow those singers to utilize their breathing technique, as they formerly did. See my latest, 2006 vocal manual—*The Art of Singing on the Breath Flow. soon to be "Electronically published by Branden Books, along with all of my other vocal manuals. www.brandenbooks.com*

A comparison of the breathing needs

A good way to understand the proper use the breathing technique is to *clarify the differences between ordinary breathing needs and those necessary for singing.* Besides the necessary physiological function for *sustaining life,* the breath supplies the *motor force* for speech and singing. With a voice, free from impediments, the motor force of the breath's contributions functions automatically and rather unconsciously. Consciousness of the need to control the breath usually starts with the first attempt to sing.

Normal speech patterns do not require the power and sustaining factors of the breath force as does singing. Since ordinary conversation is usually held at a close range, the individuals involved may pause and breathe, if shortness of breath is experienced. When singing, however, *it is necessary* to project and control the volume level of the singing voice, and conform to certain precise rhythmic patterns.

Breath & Diaphragm—the major components of the motor force

Because the singing voice is a sound-producing instrument it must have a motor force to operate. The production of vocal sound requires a steady stream of expired air, just as the wind instruments of the orchestra do. Breathing is generally thought of as a simple process of allowing the lungs to draw in air, then use that air to generate tone. But the lungs *are not* the sole motor agent of a superior breathing technique. Due to their elasticity, the lungs may be moved outward with expansion of the thoracic cage, and sink inward with exhalation.

However, when singing, the diaphragm is the main motive force and its action should be considered dominant. Certain accessory forces, such as the expansion of the coastal cage, in a lateral direction, also play an effective part in meeting the *shifting needs* of the breath support. This is especially true when taking a quick *"catch breath"*. This system of using the diaphragm, expanding the coastal cage, and lower floating ribs is generally referred to as *low breathing.* It is the only correct method of meeting all motor requirements of breath necessary for singing.

Inhalation

Under correct singing circumstances, the double-domed diaphragm descends. This allows the thoracic space to enlarge in a vertical direction. The reduced pressure created in the thoracic cavity causes an inrush of air, in order to equalize the pressure. The air distends the lungs, filling the thorax completely, and the process of inhalation has been accomplished. To experience the fullest inhalation that the lungs are capable of, try the following experiment.

While lying down *(without a pillow),* open the mouth in a *yawning position* and inhale slowly. Avoid moving the chest unnecessarily. Place your clasped hands over your diaphragm *(located under the lowest rib, and all around the waistline),* and observe the natural rising and falling action which occurs, simultaneously with the respiratory cycle. Then, in a standing position, normal for singing, try to repeat the same experience observed, as when reclining, endeavoring to accomplish a similar inhalation of air, while observing the vertical descent of the diaphragm, as the air is slowly drawn into the lungs.

Inhalation supplies the lungs with breath which, when "held in" or "back" within the lungs, automatically builds up *breath pressure* within them. This built-up breath pressure *must not* be dissipated, since it is critical in producing the motor force, which sets the vocal cords into a vibratory action, which occurs simultaneously with the outgoing cycle of exhalation. The outgoing cycles of breathing must occur slowly. The built-up air pressure within the lungs must be maintained up to the last moment of a given tone's duration.

The inhalation should be accomplished without muscular exaggeration, however the singer, in the beginning of his training, must learn how to inhale an exaggerated amount of air. The diaphragm should never be forced downward, nor upward, but should respond naturally to the slow process of taking air into the lungs, and filling them. Then afterwards, allowing the air to exit the lungs *while simultaneous producing the vibrato action of the vocal cords*, with the selected tone. Inhalation represents the *rest period* in the respiration cycle, since there is no need to maintain pressure in the lungs, as is necessary with exhalation. Exhalation represents the *work period* of the respiration cycles.

Exhalation

The act of exhalation, under normal conditions, is automatic and unconscious. When singing, however, the breath pressure that has been built up in the lungs by the inhalation must be consciously *prolonged. The vibrato* of the vocal cords *is correct and is indigenous to singing.* It must *not* be confused with a *tremolo* or a *wobble.* These negative terms are frequently mistakenly used to describe other negative functions of the singing voice, when the singer has not been properly trained, which have nothing to do with the production of the vibrato action.

The vibratory action of the vocal cords is created when the singer directs the breath pressure upward, from the lungs, through the wind pipe, toward the vocal cords. The breath pressure travels towards the vocal cords in the form of a narrow, intense stream of air, known as "the breath flow". The vocal cords respond to the breath pressure being applied to them and make an adjustment to it, positioning their edges parallel to one another. The applied breath pressure blows the parallel positioned vocal cords edges open and closed in a rapid, repetitive movement resulting in a vibratory motion known as *vibrato.* During this process, the vocal cords *do not* remain in a rigidly fixed position, but yield to the intensified stream of breath flow, being exerted against them. The air, escaping from the lungs, *does not gush out all at once*. It is released in a series of "quick, short puffs", completing the cycle of exhalation, while simultaneously producing the vibrato action.

This *vibrato action* is frequently, *though erroneously*, called "*resonance*". The frequency at which the vocal cords vibrate establishes the desired pitches. This, added to tone amplification, through mentally and physically adjusting the muscles of the falsetto tone to any of the five vowels shapes, *u (oo), i (ee), e (eh), o (oh), or a (ah)*, located in one of the resonance cavities, results in a singing tone, accompanied by a vowel.

Try the following experiment. Take a toy balloon and fill it with air. Then, with the thumb and forefingers of both hands, pull the balloon's opening taut, in a purse-string fashion. Now, manipulate the balloon's opening so that the escaping air produces a whistling or hissing sound. This illustrates how the *breath flow*, passing outward through the vocal cords, in quick, short puffs, produces a sound with the balloon, similar to the vibrato of the singing voice.

"Breath Control"

While singing, the exhalation cycle of breath flow must be controlled and *prolonged* to maintain musical timing. This is done *indirectly* with the aid of the diaphragm.

Once the vibrato action has started it becomes a reflex action and is beyond further voluntary control. *The indirectness of control must be emphasized.* During various training phases, the correct amount of breath pressure for tone production varies with the relative state of the muscles of the register being developed, and the area of the range being exercised. Each of these individual factors requires different amounts of breath pressure to produce the same note. Incidentally, a "light, lyric voice" may produce a certain pitch with minimal effort, while a *"heavy, dramatic"* voice may require twice the amount of breath pressure energy to produce the same note.

The critical moment of transferring the breath tension

While singing, and at the end of inhalation, just before starting a selected tone, there exists a moment of "breath suspension". Since inhalation and exhalation cannot function simultaneously, *the critical moment of transferring the breath tension* from the *inhalation cycle* to the *exhalation cycle* occurs, just at the end of the inhalation cycle. At that moment, the singer urgently feels the need to exhale, so he must quickly start the exhalation cycle, by directing the "pent-up air" with his lungs toward his vocal cords. They respond by vibrating, while simultaneously allowing the air maintained within the lungs to gradually dissipate. The important thing is, to catch *the exact moment* of transfer of the breath, from the intake cycle to the outgoing cycles before the tension of the breath, retained in the lungs, is dissipated. Faulty timing affects the smoothness of exhalation, the purity of tone, and control.

After a certain timing skill has been gained, this process becomes automatic. A quick, outward protrusion in the abdominal area is felt *before* each *new breath* is taken.

The forthcoming *falsetto exercises do not* require as much breath pressure as later on, when one exercises the *mixed voice* and the *full voice*. This means that the diaphragm, with its motor force controls, *is not* fully utilized until the development of the registers has advanced and the power of the chest voice has been added to that of the developed falsetto.

The shoulders and chest should remain relaxed and passive when breathing. *All breathing activity must be confined to the abdominal area, <u>downward.</u> The lowest ribs will act as the dividing line, above which there must occur <u>little or no movement.</u> When adding breath intensity to any given falsetto tone being exercised, this "low breathing" method must be constantly sought after and applied, until the correct habit of "supporting" has become ingrained.*

Should one breathe through the mouth or nose, while singing?

While singing one should breathe through the mouth! The reason that one must do so, is to refill the lungs quickly, and to adjust the "*vowel throat position* " of the forthcoming vowel and pitch to the next throat position. If one pauses to take a breath through the nose, one would be obliged to close their mouth. Doing so would *undo* the correct *vowel-throat-position of the presently sung vowel* and the *correct alignment of the registers*. The thought of chopping phrases, by pausing for quick sniff-breaths through the nose, is both incorrect and illogical.

The most <u>undesirable</u> method of breathing

The *faultiest* way of breathing for singing, is one that forbids correct tone production, and it is *shallow intercostal method* of breathing. Instead of the diaphragm being expanded downward and outward, it is *incorrectly inverted upward,* instead, and the entire chest cavity and the shoulders raised. This method allows *only a partial filling of the lungs* and interferes completely with the correct function of the vocal apparatus. The singer, gulping for air, raises his upper ribs, clavicle and shoulders, which produces tensions that forbid correct thoracic expansion and the proper lowering and outward extension of the diaphragm. "Superior breathing" depends on coordinating the muscular staying power of exhalation. When it is correctly executed there is never a deficiency of breath but rather some to spare, left in the lungs. It is important that before a new breath is taken, *all air, remaining with in the lungs, must first be expelled.*

Breathing exercises?

Student-singers who have difficulty in sustaining certain notes are often instructed to practice breathing exercises, *while they are not actually singing*. To attempt to exercise the breathing apparatus, *while not singing*, is futile. There is a popular misconception that by filling the lungs to their fullest capacity with air then slowly blowing it outward the singer will achieve greater breath capacity and sustaining power, while singing. It *is not* by expelling the air built up within lungs and "blowing it out" that one achieves a good breathing technique, but by detaining the breath within the lungs, thereby creating breath tension, the motor force of singing, then directing it against the vocal cords, and allowing it to simultaneously accomplish exhalation and vocal tone. The master teachers of the past instructed their students to "…let the vocal cords sing"!

To improve the breathing technique, the singer must strengthen the muscles of the vocal registers so that they can assist the vocal cords to tolerate increased amounts of breath tension. The more the registers accept these increased amounts of breath pressure, the stronger the singer's breathing system grows and becomes more efficient.

The most beneficial way to gain diaphragmatic strength and increase the lungs' capacity, is by singing songs *(and operatic arias),* that are slow and sustained. While singing such *"slow paced musical pieces",* the singer must pay strict attention to the evenness of his intonation and the purity of his vowels and the steady prolongation of the tone, as the breath slowly departs from the lungs.

Bodily exercises *(aerobics),* are a great help in developing the singer's breath capacity because they help maintain proper blood circulation and increase energy. Proper diet, plus sufficient sleep, is also of paramount importance. Remember, the breathing technique must always appear natural, but not necessarily silent. But it must not detract from the singer's appearance, or the dramatic meaning of the music being performed.

CHAPTER FOUR

The "Voice Building" Process
The preferred register for beginning vocal exercises

For the first vocal exercises, it is best to use the pitches of the upper register because it has been frequently neglected. When considering information from a vocal manual, the student should evaluate all new information *by comparing it to his past vocal experience*. From a *psychological* point of view, his *vocal past* has an enormous influence upon how he can best understand and utilize the new, current ideas. From a *physiological* viewpoint, he must take into account that the muscles of his voice *have already* been trained in a certain way, *often incorrectly*. That factors must certainly exert a negative effect upon how new, correct muscular arrangements must be dealt with, and changed.

A series of descending scales, practiced with tones of the upper register

It is important to clarify why the first exercises must be executed *exclusively* in a descending direction. The *descending scale patterns favor* the muscular controls of the *head register* and gives their gradual development a new advantage. They also "purify" the upper register, so that all its tones become muscularly harmonious with one another, and eventually, free from negative interrelationship with the *chest register*. In that pure state, the upper register tones can be *"detached"* from the solid, vibrant action of the lower register. The upper register's muscular controls can also be made to encompass all the tones of the singer's complete vocal range, and eventually accomplish a harmonious unification of all the tones of the singer's complete range, and position them all within *protective arc* of the head voice's muscular controls.

While descending the vocal range from its top, the singer will arrive at the registers' break *(located between E♮ and F♮, above middle C)*. At that point, he must continue downward, passing through the break, *without shifting away* from the upper register's muscular control, then proceed further downward, to the tones of lower register's muscular control. This means that *the muscles of the upper register must be made to "stretch" downward over the passage tones of the registers' break, in an overlapping manner, and eventually dominate all the tones of the lower chest register.*

At the approach to the *registers' break* tones, the singer with non-collaborating vocal registers generally experiences a tendency of the chest register to *"break away"* from the head register's muscular controls, and *snap* downward to the bottom of the range. This *breaking away* is due to the fact that, at the point of the registers' break, the chest register's muscular controls are *strongest*, while the upper register's muscular controls are *weakest there*. The singer *must not surrender* to this *"breaking away"* tendency. By insistently continuing the descending scales while retaining the muscular controls of the upper register *(even if the sound of the tones is less than ideal, and the muscular sensations seemingly "unnatural" and "cramped"), the first major step towards the vocal phenomenon of "register blending" is being taken.*

With these first descending scale exercises, the best way to avoid surrendering the descending scale to the muscular controls of the lower register at the registers' break is for the singer to *reduce the volume* of these *passaggio-crossing tones* to their minimum dynamic of *p,* and to use either the u (oo) and i (ee) vowels, in their *detached,* head voice mode. Remember, the head voice i (ee) vowel's purest mode of function is frequently very difficult for many students to understand. It must be produced with a continuous, strong, free flowing stream of breath. *But the i (ee) vowel's incorrect, chest voice mode of function possesses no breath flow what so ever.*

Unlike the lower *chest register,* which *is inherently rigid and inflexible, the head register* possesses a phenomenal, ever yielding flexibility. Stretching the head voice's muscular controls downward to cover the entire lower register's range of tones will eventually transform all their muscular actions and tonal qualities. This *stretching downward, of the upper register's muscular control, takes a long time to accomplish.* A singer may quickly achieve *a falsetto quality* with all his lower, chest tones, but this falsetto quality, in itself, is not sufficient, since, the final goal is for all the chest tones to become dominated by the muscular controls of the falsetto voice.

The falsetto's muscular controls can also be extended upward to the highest attainable pitch in the singer's range, which musicality and reasonable judgment allows. On the other hand, the muscular controls of the lower chest register are *inherently restricted* to a limited range and can only be *forced* to ascend the range to E♮ above Middle C, where they reach a blockage point. Beyond that point, "power" and "resonance" can only be extended upward by force, but with detrimental consequences for the entire vocal instrument.

Any ascending scale or vocal phrase automatically and undeniably joins the action of the chest to that of the head register, but not necessarily correctly. With each rising pitch of an ascending scale, the vocal instrument demands an appropriate increase of breath tension, and the head register, acting alone, *cannot* sustain the increased breath-tension. Consequentially, the lower register is automatically pulled into action, and the two registers then operate together. But *before proper restructuring* of the entire range, the head voice register can only play a subordinate role, but, in time it must become the dominant force. *It is for this reason that we use the descending direction exclusively, during the first phase of training, to reduce the lower register participation to a minimum, and to a subordinate status.*

THE FIRST EXERCISE:

The single, sustained falsetto tone

The first vocal exercise is *the Single, Sustained Tone,* performed in the upper *falsetto* register. The best place to perform the exercise is A♭ or A♮ above middle C. But in any case, above F♮ above middle C. The goal is for the singer to make as many muscular discoveries as possible, of the physical sensations felt, as the singer passes downward in the range and through the registers' break.

At first, the vowels u (oo) and i (ee) *(when detached from all chest voice power),* must be used exclusively, because they favor the muscular controls and tonal qualities of the upper register. These two "tuning" vowels also help to purify the upper register's action, eliminating muscular conflicts. The beginner is expected to produce the vowel as clearly as possible, remembering to diminish the volume of the tone (s) at the approach to the registers' break. One of the possible physical observations the singer may make is that, these *falsetto* tones become increasingly unrelated to what is expected of the singing voice. They seems to "shrink" in throat space and become "closed" and "squat", as the singer reaches the *break area.* And, to a greater degree, once he has descended *below* the break and into the territory dominated by the chest voice. However, these "shrinking" or "closing" sensations are natural muscular responses, prior to advanced vocal structuring, which changes most the singer's perceptions.

This compromise of *"vowel and throat space"* also reveals to the singer the *actual* "inherently narrow contours" of the registers at the point of the registers' break, as opposed to how the singer perceives them, as being wide-open throat tones, *when listening to other, advanced singers singing.* Later, we will discuss how to alter these inherent narrow contours of the registers' break tones to conform to a superior structure which enables the singer to sing through the registers' break area with superior tone quality, control of all the dynamics of the breath force, vowel purity, plus greatly all those misperceived "wide open- throated tones." These descending scales serve to reduce the "weight" and "bulk" of the lower register, by holding back its volume and bulk, and allowing the thinner "falsetto" quality to dominate its tones.

There exists an enormous variety of muscular conditions in which singing voices are generally and initially found: some are completely dysfunctional and "raw", others with reasonably good functions, and others with seeming, advanced singing skills. Therefore, without actually hearing any of these singers in person, allowances must be made with the principles of this manual for each voice's individuality. Therefore, the singer should experiment with all these first exercises, and make personal judgments, based upon his own, individual vocal status.

By referring back to the section of this manual entitled *"The Mechanical Function of the Five Singing Vowels" (p. 23),* and reviewing how each vowel *tends* to inherently react, the singer becomes familiar with the muscular sensations and tonal attributes of the pitches of his own vocal range and his registers' break area, at *his* present state of development. In this way, he will be able to compare and evaluate how the registers' break tones change, when each new structural rule is applied to them, and how their change effects all the remaining tones of his range.

It is beneficial to mention here that many individuals erroneously believe that a singer's vocal category—*tenor, baritone, or bass*—is based solely upon its initial *"color" and/or "timbre"* and potential range of singable, quality tones. *This method is incorrect and unreliable.* The *correct basis* upon which a singing voice is accurately categorized, is the inherent size and strength of the muscles of both vocal registers, individually, which are only revealed, after a certain amount of time has past. *Basses and baritones possess inherently larger-sized, stronger muscles in their lower registers*, compared to the inherent size and muscular strength of their upper registers. Tenors *possess inherently larger and stronger upper register muscles, than lower register muscles.*

When structuring tenor voices, one of the most beneficial concepts is to understand that before *re*structuring, the male singer's lower register *disadvantageously contains* a greater number of lower register tones than upper register tones. But in time, most of those lower tones, prove to be "unusable" and "antagonistic" towards the tones of the Registers' Break and the Top Range. Because of this "imbalance", it is imperative to give the fewer "head voice tones" preferential treatment, so that they may reveal to the singer how their progressive development influences the development of his lower register. This preferential treatment of the upper register is the only reliable way *for a singer to understand his true vocal category.* Accurately categorizing a singing voice is not a straightforward nor quick task, when the upper register's tones have been neglected. It is only after the upper register's tones have been given priority of development that the tenor voice reveals its proper "weight", "tonal color", and most importantly, its permanently and "stable" lower tones. This structural approach simultaneously reveals other critical musical factors, such as evenness of the vocal line, purity of vowels, beauty of tone, and control of all the breath-dynamics.

With all the above in mind, it can be understood how most of the structural problems which beginner-tenors encounter can be solved by correctly restructuring the *upper middle* and *top sections* of their vocal ranges first. Specifically, the *passage* tones from middle C to the E♮ above it, and all tones above F♮, above middle C and upward. These forthcoming, structural exercises deal exclusively with *falsetto tones* which possess *no vibrato action.*

The *vibrato action* is created by the vocal cords, when breath tension is applied to them, but with these first exercises, the singer will be dealing with tones that *do not* possess any *vibrato action,* nor strong, "resonant", "projecting" qualities, that are generally associated with a professional voice. Suspension of judgment, during this early period of training, is one of the most important factors necessary for achieving a superior singing instrument. It is also a test of the singer's *patience,* and his *logic.* Detailed explanations will be provided later, which clarify how the upper register's tones become transformed, and allow for an accurate determination of the tenor's true vocal category of *"lyric"*, *"spinto", or "dramatic"*. These determinants will be the "weight" of the voice, and the number of notes that can be permanently added to the singer's complete singing range, that can be drawn from the lower register's "power system". Whatever number of tones those lower notes turn out to be, they must possess clear, pure vowels, beauty of tone, and grant the singer control of all the breath-dynamics, especially with the *passaggio* tones.   Now for the first exercises.

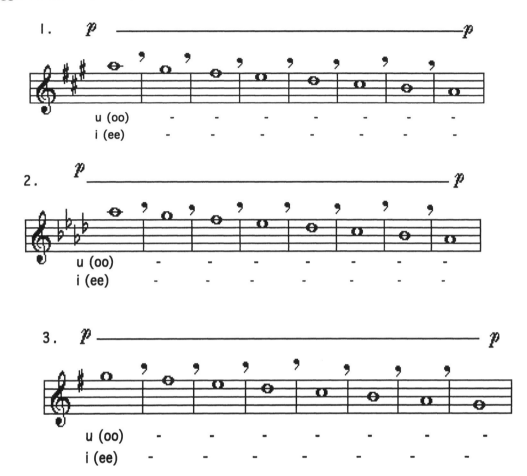

Above are three sets of single, sustained, upper register, detached falsetto tone exercises. They are to be performed with the "head voice" vowels u (oo) and i (ee), and without a vibrato action. Then, much later with the e (eh), o (oh), and a (ah) vowels, and in a descending direction. It is important to remember that the tenor range is actually located an octave below the tones that are presently written into all music scores *(see pgs. 31 & 32)*.

It is not unusual for the tenor voice to respond in such a positive way to these first "detached falsetto" tones that his voice "zooms" unexpectedly and uncontrollably upward, away from the chest voice, toward high C, with a soprano-like sound, If that occurs, the singer should note the purity of these high-zooming, "soprano like" "falsetto" tones, and utilize their sounds and vocal actions, as the standard of purity *that all his other falsetto tones should possess*. It is advisable to do some personal experimentation with these exercises, by lowering and raising their keys a bit, and observing how your voice responds.

One of the important things, which every superior singers eventually learn about singing voice voices is that, it *seem* to "talk to him"; that is to say, it frequently "suggests" to him, through physical sensations, what is "good" or "bad", "safe" or "unsafe" for the muscles of his singing instrument. This kind of "voice communication" will be discussed later.

The importance of understanding the "detached" falsetto

More than all other singers, *the tenor* must develop a precise understanding of the *"detached state" (detached from the chest voice)*, of his upper register's falsetto tones, which we use for exercising his singing instrument, and maintaining its health. *It is only from this "detached state" that the singer progresses to other superior states of vocal development, throughout his career.* The *detached falsetto* tone, submitted to gradual increases of breath tension, slowly develops strength and eventually "connects" itself *(with the singer's instigation),* to the muscular activities of the *chest voice.* Once the detached falsetto has been *attached* to the chest voice, *the singer must be also capable of detaching it from all connection to the chest voice.* This is a process and skill that is best learned slowly. Later it can be performed with great spontaneity and agility.

Vowel Throat-Sockets (or throat arrangements)

Each and every combination of *pitch and vowel*, within the singer's complete range, *possesses its own individual vowel-throat-socket.* By making the upper register, and all of its *vowel-throat-sockets,* become the dominant muscular control throughout the complete range, then stressing each individual pitch's vowel-socket, through the application of progressively-increased amounts of breath tension, each pitch may be eventually developed to its maximum potential. In this way, the singer can eventually match all the developed tones of the upper register's vowel throat-sockets to the corresponding vowel throat-sockets of the lower register's tones, creating a *synergism,* or *team of both registers*. Doing so eliminates the inherent antagonism between the two registers, and subjugates them to the singer's control. Then, he may sing with precise muscular intonation and control, and superior tonal quality.

Each vowel's individual influence upon a tone

Each of the five vowels throat-sockets, when in the *connected mode* of singing, *(when both chest and head voice are connective to each other)*, contributes its own individual muscular influence upon a selected tone. This can be experienced if one selects a pitch, then performs the *permanent sequence of vowels, starting with the u (oo) vowel, then passing on to the i (ee) vowel, then the e (eh) vowel, then the o (oh) vowel and finally arriving at the a (ah) vowel, without* taking a new breath in between these vowels. After the voice has reached an advanced state of development, known of as "open throat singing", the passage of the five vowel are assigned a different orders, to serve the singer to sing his full range of tones with harmony and precision. This will be explained later. *For now*, the passage through the five vowels must be performed in the order mentioned above. When the singer finds difficulty with the ideal passage through the five vowels, he make perform a less demanding version of them, separating them into two separate groups; *group one* the u (oo), o (oh), and a (ah) vowels, and the *second group,* the i (ee) and e (eh) vowels, performing each group at a separate me.

The chart below can be very useful, as vocal imagery, to guide the singer in identifying certain aspects of muscular behavior from others. Once the singer leaves the first vowel *u (oo)* and changes it to the *i (ee)* vowel, there occurs an automatic and undeniable increase of lower register's muscular participation with the tone being sung. A further The above increase occurs when applying the *e (eh)* vowel, and still more increases occur with the *o (oh),* until the *a (ah)* vowel is reached, where upon, the maximum participation of the lower register occurs.

The u (oo) vowel	=	0%	of lower register muscular participation.
The i (ee) vowel	=	25%	of lower register muscular participation.
The e (eh) vowel	=	50%	of lower register muscular participation.
The o (oh) vowel	=	75%	of lower register muscular participation.
The a (ah) vowel	=	100%	of lower register muscular participation.

For theoretical purposes, let us assign each individual vowel a 25% value *(after departing from the u (oo) vowel—the purest and most "detached" of the five vowels—when it is not connected to the power of the chest voice),* so that the total of these four vowels makes up 100% of the lower register's muscular participation.

Although these percentages may not be scientifically precise, undeniably, there is a considerable increase of lower register muscular participation with each vowel change. The *reverse* is true when a tone is started with the *a (ah) vowel,* wherein the fullest connection of the lower register to the upper register is immediately and already operative. With the a (ah), the work load for producing the tone is at its highest level. When the singer establishes a tone with the *a (ah)* vowel and changes it to an *o (oh)* vowel, then to an *e (eh),* then to an *i (ee)* arriving finally at the *u (oo)* vowel, the singer can graphically understand the gradual, progressive reductions of the chest voice's muscular participation with each succeeding vowel, and the chest voice participation's *total deduction* when arriving at the *u (oo)* vowel. The beginner should not become anxious, if this seems complex and overly mechanical. With repeated references to, and subsequent applications of these concepts, it will all become easier to understand.

THE SECOND VOCAL EXERCISE:
<u>Descending falsetto scales that include vocal movement</u>

After a certain period of experimentation with the *1st exercise, The Single Sustained Tones,* the singer should then perform some new exercises that include vocal movement. This leads to *the second basic exercise* for structuring the singing instrument: *Descending, Detached Falsetto Scales* that possess more than one pitch and include vocal movement.

The purpose of the new exercises is twofold: *1)* to gain experience with the use of the upper register's muscular controls *while incorporating vocal movement*; and *2)* to continue the process of overlapping the detached falsetto muscular controls downward in the range, over all the tones of the lower register, *while denying the lower register's natural vibrato action or "core brilliance."*

Carrying out these instructions may cause the singer a great deal of confusion and insecurity. Many frustrated singers permanently decide to eliminate the use of these detached falsetto exercises. This is so because they temporarily deny the singer the resonant elements of the lower register, which are more readily identifiable and stable, even if incorrect, and associated with the *"performing voice",* than is the *vague nature* of the transitory, progressively developing, detached falsetto tones. When the singer is denied the solidity and vibrancy of the lower register, he often feels confused and discouraged. However, the "vagueness" is only *temporary,* in order to allow the *chest register* to undergo the necessary transformation from its initial dominance to a state of subordination to, and cooperation with the muscles of the upper register.

The singer must trust that, with the passing of time and advanced development of the detached falsetto voice, superior and tangible vocal controls will present themselves. For a long period, the detached falsetto exercises may create an impression for the singer, that his voice is being muffled, or described more traditionally, *"covered"* and that it is *"shrinking"* and has become fragmented. These are merely early symptoms that will change in time—especially when the contributions of the chest voice are added to the developed falsetto. In the mean time, with the continued use of the detached falsetto, these beneficial, but misunderstood qualities, spread downward from the top range and influence the singer's lower range in a positive manner, but *they slowly become less confusing and intimidating,* to understand.

This "veiled or covered quality", mentioned above is only temporary, and perceived more acutely by the singer, than by his listeners. These influences upon the developing voice *must not* be sacrificed in order to prematurely apply the core brilliance and projecting volume of the chest voice to any of these detached falsetto controlled tones. That would be too soon, and a great mistake. With great patience, and with the use of the forthcoming exercises of the *messa di voce (p. 78)*. These falsetto tones will eventually reach a more advanced stable state of development. Then, all the missing core brilliance and desired projecting power will emerge, but in a new, correct and permanent form. They will grant the singer full control of dynamics, pure vowels, and a superior, professional tone quality. It is helpful for the singer to remember that the results of all exercises, simple or complex, _cannot_ be understood within the same time period time in which they are being performed. Therefore, it is advisable to allow at least a day or more to pass, resting the voice completely. Then, attempt to sing, *not* vocalize and observe the results. Only then will the singer come to understand the positive results attained by any and all exercises that have been correctly applied.

Below are *three sets of descending scale exercises*, which include vocal movement. They are to be performed with the *detached falsetto*, slowly and with strict attention paid to the *legato* application. These scales should be raised and lowered a tone or two, to encompass as much of the complete vocal range as possible.

Descending scales using detached falsetto, upper register tones

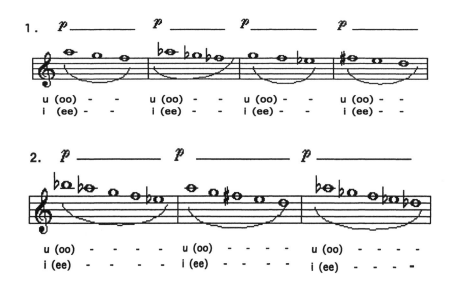

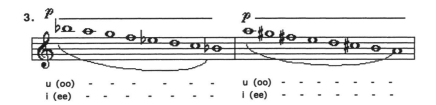

Try these above, descending scales. Use a breathy u (oo) vowel, then a breathy i (ee) vowel. Remember, the tenor's range is an octave lower than where these scales are written.

These descending scales help the singer become familiar with the various throat sensations experienced, when approaching the registers' break from above it, passing over it, and descending further downward in the range, while endeavoring to encompass all the tones of the chest voice, with the detached falsetto's muscular controls.

While descending the scale from the head voice register, as the singer approaches the first tone of the chest register, E♮ above middle C, the breath stream may attempt to break away from the head voice's control and switch itself over to the muscular control of the chest register. This is *not* desirable and the singer *must resist this*. If this should happened, the singer should stop the exercise, rest his voice for a while, then make another attempt at descending the range from above the registers' break, and overlap all these "break tones" with the detached falsetto's muscular controls. Take several rest periods, and repeat the process several times again. Eventually, control of these "break tones" will gradually be *taken away from the muscular controls of the lower register* and *reassigned to the muscular controls of the upper register*. After this has been accomplished, these *converted*, lower range tones may possess a "muffled" or "covered" quality, and become rather unstable, for quite some time.

These qualities are correct and appropriate to them, and temporary. The singer should not try bring the core brilliance of the lower register back into them, otherwise, the falsetto tones will not develop further. Eventually the falsetto will reach an advanced stage of strength and own its own "invite" the core brilliance to join the falsetto tone, but it will remain dominated by the falsetto's muscular controls. The singer must also be able to remove the newly invited "core brilliance" from the tone, at will. The newly added *core brilliance*, when added to any developed falsetto tone, must forever remain subjected to the dominant controls of the advanced detached falsetto voice. At that advanced stage of development the falsetto develops into the *mezzo-falso*—best known as the *"mixed voice" (p. 79)*.

Legato: *The meaning of the term*

With the introduction of movement into these above exercises, the term *legato* must be explained. Generally, *legato* is considered to be a method of closely connecting two or more tones of a vocal phrase, when passing from one to another, so as *not* to allow any audible gaps in sound. Without denying that is the desired goal of legato singing, there exist many more critical factors to the understanding and performance of a correct legato maneuver. In their pursuit of legato, most singers concentrate their efforts solely upon the tonal results, while failing to consider the causative factors that achieve successful legato. Therefore, their "mental imagery" is partial, and they lack clear understanding of the "breath pressure" requirements.

Exercise scales generally employ but a single vowel. Conversely, a vocal phrase contains many vowels "scrambled" into the text, and out of their ideal order—u (oo), i (ee), e (eh), o (oh), and a (ah). Achieving legato, while exercising the voice is a vastly different matter than when singing a musical piece, which presents a much greater challenge.

During the performance of a single, sustained note whose words present different vowel arrangements, the intensity of breath stream, when passing from one vowel to the next, must not be dissipated, not even for a second. *Vibrato* and breath-flow must harmoniously coexist, since they are co-dependent. When passing from one vowel to the next, the breath flow, established on the first tone, and its vowel, must be reduced and transferred to the upper note, and its new vowel, then rapidly increased again, appropriately to the second note, and its vowel.

When executing a *descending* phrase, the reverse happens; the singer establishes the top note and its particular vowel, reduces the breath flow, then rapidly moves downward to the note below and its particular vowel, where he quickly adjusts the breath flow and the vowel's throat socket, appropriately, in order to sing the lower note. However, with this descending movement, the singer must quickly diminish the intensity of the breath, to accurately establish the accuracy of the lower note, but he must not to add an inappropriate amount of breath pressure, or it will bring into play an excessive amount of chest voice weight and thickness.

"True Legato" is only possible when each individual tone in the singer's range *has been individually strengthened* to a state of muscular perfection. In such a state, no tone is weak and/or incapable of rapidly reducing and/or increasing the intensity of the breath flow, when passing from one tone and its particular vowel, to the next note and its particular vowel, as is demanded by correct legato singing.

The vowels employed on adjacent tones of a selected tone have a critical influence upon how one approaches the transfer of the breath flow from one tone to the next one. There is a *positive* influence upon the legato, when passing from a lower tone to a higher tone, when both vowels are *open* vowels—such as the (o) oh) vowel and a (ah) vowels. But there is a *difficulty* when passing from a lower tone to a higher tone, when the lower vowel is a *closed* vowel—u (oo) or i (ee)—and the upper tone's vowel is an *open* vowel, such as an open o (oh) or *fully open* (ah) vowel.

The u (oo), o (oh), and a (ah) vowels tens to remain *"open throated"*, for the entire length of the *resonance channel*, from bottom to top, so that breath flow may easily flow upward and downward within it. With the "closed" i (ee) and e (eh) vowels, the *resonance channel* tends to *"close"* and deny the breath from flowing along its entire length. Therefore, it is useful for the singer to always assure that when singing the i (ee) and e (eh) vowels *he does not stop the breath flow.*

Note: The *"portamento"* is frequently used to accommodate the passage from one note to another, when the *bottom note* is sung with a closed i (ee) vowel, and the *top note* is sung with an open vowel, such as an a (ah). The *portamento* is a method by which the singer carries the i (ee) vowel of the lower note upward to the top note, pauses briefly there, then changes the top note from its "portamented" i (ee) vowel to the upper note's originally assigned a (ah) vowel. The *portamento* is employed in order to maintain an open throated position *(of the resonance tract),* when passing from a *closed vowel* such as u (oo) or i (ee), to an *open vowel* such as o (oh) or a (ah) in order to facilitate and maintain the free flow of breath.

The distance between the lower note and the upper note also critically effects the manner in which correct legato can be accomplished. It is more difficult to maintain legato when singing *widely-spaced notes*, than it is with *closely-spaced notes*. Success with the *portamento* involves skill in perpetuating the breath flow, while moving from the pitch sung with a closed vowel, to the pitch sung with and open vowel, and *vice versa.*

The unusual lower octave of all correctly structured singing voices, and the "head voice ramp"

Most singers are unaware of the unusual, but necessary functions of the lower octave of all singer's voices. Traditionally, ascending scales are applied to the lower tones of the singer's range using the *"raw"* chest voice a (ah) vowel, *(no matter how incorrect or vague their purpose)*, with the intention of building *"solid tone"* and *"extending"* the range upward. At first, some voices appear to respond rather well to these ascending scales which *later on* prove to have been harmful. The *"raw"*, *"unblended"*, or *"unmixed"* a (ah) vowel, meaning the a (ah) vowel when it has *not been combined* with the protective muscular controls of the upper register immediately defeats the success of all ascending scales.

Here are some comments about the *"raw, "unblended"* a (ah) vowel, by two of the greatest singer/voice teachers of the past, and of all times.

Lilli Lehman's comments on "the a (ah) vowel, of former days".

"The Italians, who sing well, *never speak or sing the vowel sound ah,* otherwise than *mixed,* and only the *neglect of this mixture* could have brought the decadence of the Italian teaching of song. The *ah,* as sung by the Italians of the present-day, is quite flat, and sounds commonplace, almost like an affront. It can range itself, that is connect itself, with no other vowel, makes all vocal connections impossible, evolves very ugly registers, and, lying low in the throat, summons forth no palatal resonance. The power of contraction of the muscles of speech *(dominated by the negative, unmixed a (ah) vowel),* is insufficient, and this insufficiency misleads the singer to constrict the throat muscles, which are not trained to the endurance of it. The fatal tremolo is always the result of this manner of singing." —*1902*

Lillie Lehmann (1848-1929) was described by *Jean de Reske* as " the greatest artist of the century." She sang altogether 170 roles, ranging from coloratura to Wagnerian heroines. She sang at the first Bayreuth Festival, and sang *Isolde* in Vienna as late as 1090, when she was 61. She was instrumental in establishing the Salzburg Festival, and was later its artistic director. At the age of seventy, she was still appearing before the public as a Lieder singer.

Giovanni Sbriglia's comments on the English a (ah) vowel.

"More American voices are ruined by being training on the *English "ah"* than any other way. It gives an open flat-topped voice. Even great singers get this open voice, from fatigue. Use loose, protruding lips with the proper breath support to cure this common fault."

Giovanni Sbriglia (1832-1916), a Neapolitan tenor, made his debut at the San Carlo Theater of Naples, in Italy, in 1853, and in New York in 1860 at the Academy of Music with *Adelina Patti* in *La Sonnabula.* He toured the United States with other artists, and sang in Mexico and Cuba. After his European career, he settled in Paris in 1875, where he became an historical teacher of singing. Among his students were *Jean and Eduard de Reszke, Pol Plaçon, Lillian Nordica, and Sybil Sanderson.* It was under his tutelage that *Jean de Reszke* most successfully changed from baritone to tenor.

The process of overlapping the entire lower register's tones with the advanced development of the upper register's falsetto tones, and temporarily neglecting the "raw" a (ah) vowel completely and utilizing both the detached falsetto *aw,* u (oo), and i (ee) vowels, can create a kind of *"ramp"* upon which the power of the lower register travels, when performing all ascending vocal movement. This ramp, or tract, is physiologically positioned vertically in the singer's throat. Its *lower section* located in the singer's lower throat channel, its *middle section* located at the posterior area of the mouth-pharynx cavity, and its *top section* leading upward in the range to the sinus and head cavities.

This *vertically-positioned vocal ramp* is shaped like the inner curve of the letter C. When the controls of the upper register are *not* structurally created and carried downward to cover all the tones of the lower octave, *this critically important "vocal ramp" will be missing.* Consequently, the only recourse the singer has is to *"push upward"* in the range the unrefined, *thick negative power* of the chest register.

When the entire vocal "ramp" has been structured to perfection, all vocal movement, in both ascending and descending directions, is always performed with the muscular controls of *both registers* (never with one single register), with a mixture of the controls of both registers. This is the only way that all tones of the *lower octave* will function in permanent harmony with the tones of the *upper octave* of the vocal range. There are other important reasons why the upper register's muscular controls must overlap the entire lower register. Such as: the process of matching the vowel/throat-sockets of the lower octave to those of the upper octave. That can only be accomplished after structuring the upper portion of the "vocal tract" *first*. Until the long-term process of "stretching" downward and strengthening the action of the upper register's muscular controls is accomplished, there is no hope for the singer to achieve a musically functioning ascending scale of vocal phrase.

"Power" and *"core brilliance",* drawn from the muscular actions of the "raw" chest voice, must never be allowed to function independently, in any part of the vocal range, but must be "restrained" and "attached" to the controls of the upper register. Prior to proper structuring, these upper register controls are inoperative in the lower octave, and must be *calculatingly* established there.

Once the upper tones of the falsetto register, F♮ above middle C, upward to high C, have reached advanced development, they create an *upward pulling action*—pulling all the tones of the complete range in an opposite direction from the lower chest register. This *"upward pull"* is used to help the ascending movement of all vocal scales and phrases. While the developed upper register's tones tend to pull upward, away from the chest voice, the *chest register* tends to pull *downward,* away from the upper register. This lower register's behavior is also correct, and the singer must utilize its downward pulling, muscular action in order to counter the upward pull of the upper register. These upward and downward pulls of both registers are the only manner by which the singer can properly control the ascending and descending movements of his voice.

As the muscles controlling the falsetto tones progressively develop strength, they *"invite"* the vibrato and *"projecting power"* of the lower register to join them in the production of all basic tone. The initial, separate timbres of both registers come to match each other in "sound" and "muscular action" throughout the entire range. During each "warm up" session, when the singer is preparing the "slumbering" voice for singing, his first tones must be started with the purest, *softest detached-falsetto tone, preferably an u (oo) vowel that is then changed into an o (oh) vowel, then an a (ah) vowel.* This a(ah) vowel tone can then be swelled to "invite" the vibrato action and "power" of the lower register to join it.

There are relatively few exercises in this manual. However, none should be considered less important than any other one. None of them should be considered of "transitory use". They are the *permanent tools* which efficiently and correctly establish and maintain superior vocal usage and vocal health, for the singer's vocal lifetime.

The "resonance channel," or the "colonna sonora", as it was termed by the old Italian Teachers

When it is stated that the singing instrument must be "built", it means that the singer must arrange, through selected exercises, the entire vocal range, or *resonance channel*, tone by tone, as well as strengthen each individual tone. This *resonance channel* was called the "*colonna sonora",* by the early master Italian teachers. The sound waves *(vibrato)* emanating from the vocal cords, must travel backward and upward in the posterior area of the mouth-pharynx cavity, then freely up and down the "*colonna sonora*", then further upward, behind both the soft and hard palates, into the nasal and head-cavities, and terminating at specific "hook up" points, along the way, then resonate within them.

This *resonance channel* must be created *from top-to-bottom*, instead of *from bottom-to-top*, using the structuring experiences gained at the top of the range as a model for structuring the middle and lower sections of the vocal range.

All musical instruments require a mandatory dual-coupling system, a scientific law in which the originator of the pitch, *factor #1*, must be coupled with a corresponding resonator, *factor #2*. The violin, whose strings, bowed by the players fingers, generate the original vibrations of its tones, *factor #1*, must couple with the terminal resonator points inside the wooden, resonator chamber of the instrument, *factor #2*. The trumpet, whose mouthpiece, along with the trumpeter's lips, serves as the generator of the originating pitches, *factor #1*, must be coupled with their terminal resonating points along the passageway of the main body of the instrument, *factor #2*.

This "dual-coupling system" law is *also applicable* to the singing instrument. The vocal cords, *factor #1*, which produce the solid, projecting vibrato action of all superior singing tones must couple with *factor #2*, the hookup points, located within the various resonating cavities of the mouth-pharynx, sinus and head cavities.

Through the successful execution of the *messa di voce* exercise, the barrier between the registers which, before the proper structuring, *prohibits* the solid, brilliant power of the chest voice, *factor #1*, from coupling with the sweetness of the head voice, *factor #2*, may be permanently removed. This is accomplished by experiencing success with the *messa di voce* exercise, employing the detached falsetto i (ee) vowel, which allows the brilliant vibrato action of the chest voice, produced by the vocal cords, to " *pierce through*" the sinus tissue of the head voice muscles *(which prior to being "pierced" by the falsetto i (ee) vowel can only produce "covered" and "opaque sounds")*, and immediately "light up" every formerly "dulled" tone, from that point, and there afterwards. The brilliant vibrations of the vocal cords, may then travel freely upward along the length of *resonance channel* and arrive at their terminal "hook up" points, within any of the various resonance cavities, according to the pitch and vowel being presently sung. Once inside the appropriate resonance cavity, the vocal cords' vibrations, of the selected tone, resonate brightly and clearly.

These anatomical resonance cavities of the *lower throat channel*, the *mouth-pharynx cavity*, the nasal, and the head cavities of the skull, all of which make up the entire resonance channel, exist as a gift of nature. However, this does not mean that locating, understanding their nature and functions, and their employs their contributions to superior singing *is not* a simple matter of casual discovery, accomplished by naively performing a series of vocal scales. Discovering and understanding these resonance cavities is instead, a complex and time consuming procedure that requires specific knowledge and specific applications of certain vocal exercises.

Vocal pitch is the product of *a vibrator* having an exact length, an exact thickness, and an exact tension. Every tone of the singer's range is produced by a slightly different laryngeal-pharyngeal adjustment *(head voice/chest voice combination)*. There are many gradations in vibrator mass; in other words, different effective lengths and thickness of the vocal cords' *layers* engaged, necessary to accurately satisfy the specific laryngeal-pharyngeal conditions of each individual pitch of the singer's complete range of tones. When ascending the range, to calibrate accurate pitch changes, the vocal cords become gradually *shorter, tauter and thinner.* Conversely, when descending the range the vocal cords *lengthen, slacken, and thicken.* This is the result of individual, precise levels of *breath tension* being applied to the vocal cords, for each individual tone and its accompanying vowel, of a rising scale or vocal phrase. The "breath tension" assumes the form of *a narrow, focused, stream of concentrated breath*, applied *directly to the vocal cords.*

A strong driving force is created by the breath pressure, that has been built up within the lungs, when the singer holds back the breath for a few moments, within lungs, before launching a selected note. The vocal cords, in response to the intense, narrow stream of breath tension being focused against them, yield to it, in a bowing action. They first open, in a rapid-fire movement, allowing a puff of air to escape, then they rapidly close again, whereupon a new cycle of the same behavior is immediately initiated. In other words, the vocal cords come together, separate, come together again, and separate again, under the pressure of the breath stream. This cycle continues as long as a musical note is being prolonged, which requires of the singer, for him to supply a continuous flow of the breath stream to selected pitch and vowel, for the duration of the tone.

Below, An illustration of an *incorrect* vocal condition *(below),* showing a disconnected and wrong pathway which the rising sound waves will travel, when the upper register's help *has not* been structured into the lower range area.

For the singer to raise the pitch, the amount of breath tension being applied to the vocal cords must be proportionately *increased.* When *descending the scale,* the breath tension must be proportionately decreased. Even a beginning-singer may possess relatively easy access to the varying amounts of breath tension, that can be applied to the vocal cords. But, he *has no direct control over the adjustments of the vocal cords, where precise* length *and thickness are required. That requires that all the tones of his vocal passaggio must be restructured, by the detached, falsetto i (ee) vowel. How this is accomplished will be explained later.*

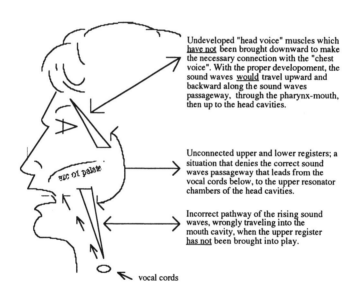

Undeveloped "head voice" muscles which <u>have not</u> been brought downward to make the necessary connection with the "chest voice". With the proper developoment, the sound waves <u>would</u> travel upward and backward along the sound waves passageway, through the pharynx-mouth, then up to the head cavities.

Unconnected upper and lower registers; a situation that denies the correct sound waves passageway that leads from the vocal cords below, to the upper resonator chambers of the head cavities.

Incorrect pathway of the rising sound waves, wrongly traveling into the mouth cavity, when the upper register <u>has not</u> been brought into play.

arc of palate

vocal cords

When the singer performs an ascending scale, b*efore the resonance channel has been properly structured*, he can easily understand the inherent, antagonism that exists between the upper and lower registers, by the difficulties he encounters in attempting to accomplish a smooth, ascent of the range, especially when he reaches the *passaggio's tones.*

Decreases and increases of the vibratory mass

We must establish that, when an ascending scale is correctly executed, there occur incremental decreases in the vibratory mass. In other words, a "shortening/thinning" process of the vocal cords occurs with each successive higher pitch. For this to be correctly accomplished, while ascending the scale, there must occur a gradual elimination of the vibrator mass. At the bottom of the singer's range, the tones must be produced with a *"longer/thicker"* vocal cords arrangement. And, at the top of the singer's range, the tones must be produced with a *"shorter/thinner"* vocal cords arrangement. This is both correct and desirable. But how is this done?

There are those who believe that the shortening-or-lengthening, thinning-or-thickening process of the vocal cords can be directly controlled by the singer, by "lightening" the voice and or/ singing "lyric repertory", for a while. And, that the process is simple, and readily accessible to. They believe that success with this process is simply a matter of discovering the right esthetic feeling in the throat. Of course this is a fantasy.

The shortening-or-lengthening, thinning-or-thickening of a singer's vocal cords *is* not readily accessible to any singer. Almost every hopeful singer who enters a vocal training program quickly realizes that, whenever he is assigned an ascending scale, and has no way of controlling the shortening-or-lengthening, thinning-or-thickening of a singer's vocal cords, the ascending scale is poorly executed, if it can be completed at all, and the quality of the scale are inferior, its vowels compromised. The only way a novice can produce the ascending scale, with his limited development, is by ineptly increasing the "breath tension", making each successive rising tone louder, but not accurate nor beautiful. Because there has been no proper structuring of the vocal tract, he can only produce a raw, unwieldy scale.

It has been discovered that the head voice muscles, *(located within the mouth-pharynx and the upper, nasal and head cavities),* are inherently "thinner" than the muscles of the chest voice, which are located in the lower tract of the *pharynx,* within the lower throat channel, which is inherently "thick". However, when the head voice muscles have taken possession of these lower note and transforms them away from their original "bulk" and "thickness", thereafter, they respond in a completely harmonious manner by matching, and fitting into the thinner muscular contours of the head voice register's range, and accomplishing, in part, the much desired shortening-or-lengthening, thinning-or-thickening process. Simultaneously, the vocal cords, accomplish the same thinning-or-thickening process, in their own particular manner, with each individual higher pitch and vowel.

When a particular tone of the "transformed chest voice" has been properly mixed with the muscular controls of the head voice, it has been transformed away from its original rigid state and has adopted a buoyant form, due to the head voice's influence of infusing any selected tone with an abundance of the breath flow. When that be the case, and the singer performs an ascending scale, continuously changing from a lower pitch to higher one, the now transformed chest voice tone no longer in a ridge state, adjusts itself away from its original thickness and to the thinness factor, because of the strong influence being exerted upon it, by the thinner size and shape of the head voice dominated resonance channel. As the singer ascends the range and switches from a lower resonance cavity, to a higher on, each resonance cavity, along the length of the resonance channel, is smaller than the previous one, which is another contributor to the thickening-thinning, shorting-or lengthening of the vocal cords' process.

This means that the resonance chamber *itself,* due to its inherent, thinner shape, plus the varying sizes of the throat-openings of each individual pitch located within its boundaries, makes yet another contribution to the success of the thinning and thickening process, while the presently sung vowel adjusts the length and/or width of the vocal cords, thereby completing the accomplish of the thickening and/or thinning process of the vocal cords, and the decreases and/or increases of the vibratory mass. You may want to read by most recent vocal manual—*The Art of Singing on the Breath Flow,* which will soon be available through my publisher, Branden Publications, Inc., on their "Branden Books" website: *www.brandenbooks.com*

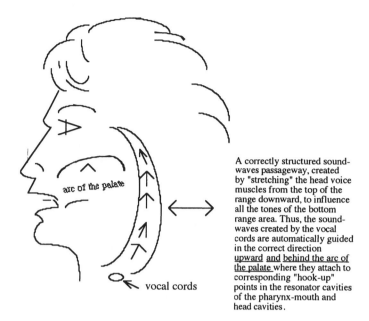

A correctly structured sound-waves passageway, created by "stretching" the head voice muscles from the top of the range downward, to influence all the tones of the bottom range area. Thus, the sound-waves created by the vocal cords are automatically guided in the correct direction upward and behind the arc of the palate where they attach to corresponding "hook-up" points in the resonator cavities of the pharynx-mouth and head cavities.

The illustration above shows *a correct* vocal condition. Here, the structured sound waves passageway leads from the vocal cords upward, backward, behind the arc of the palate, and into the resonator cavities of the posterior area of the pharynx-mouth; then further up the sound waves passageway, to attach themselves to the "hookup" points, located within the various resonance cavities. This tract, which was originally *thick* at its bottom, due to the *influences of the chest voice's muscles*, and thin at its top, *due to the influences of the head voice*, has now been transformed into a vertical ascending, curved, thinly-shaped passageway along its entire length, due to many special exercises that accomplish that long, drawn out task.

The phenomenal "adjustability" of the pharyngeal tract's muscles,

It is interesting to note that, of all living creatures, *only human beings can adjust both their pharyngeal muscles and their laryngeal together simultaneously, to produce their speaking and singing voices.* Where the singing voice is concerned, that means that, after the singer transports the influence of his head voice muscles influence all the way downward to the bottom of the chest voice's range, he can raise his larynx upward and backward toward the upper posterior area of the mouth pharynx cavity, and attach it to a selected pitch, located somewhere along the length of *laryngeal channel.* Or, said more simpler, he can connect his larynx to any tone, anywhere along the complete range of his singing voice. With all superior tenors, this connection, between the larynx and the pharynx, must first be accomplished with the pitch of Bf below middle

This technique of attaching the *larynx to the pharynx* is also possible with all the tones below B♭ below middle C. But this critical *switch over tone of* B♭ must first be structured in a particular way, in order to accomplish that. When the singer connects his larynx to his pharynx higher up in the range, with any of the tones of *E♭, E♮, F♮, and F♯, above middle C*, another major transitional, or switch-over point is reached. The act of "lifting and connecting" the larynx and pharynx to each other must also be accomplished with those tones, but that takes a greater effort, since all those pitches above the E♭ above middle C, demands a major increase of breath force, which could be easily misdirected. If that occurs, the singer risks carrying the power of his chest voice, wrongly and excessively upward in his range, into the sensitive pitches of the *passaggio,* thereby causing disruptive muscles actions with all of its tones.

This "switching from one register to another", when successfully accomplished, confirms and clarifies for the singers the fact that, the muscles of his pharyngeal-tract *(or head voice range),* possess an inherently *malleable* nature. They can be stretched downward from their original territory to the "switch over points" in various part of the singer's range. And they can also be made to conform to various predetermined shapes—which are called "vowels"—which are capable performing, for the singer, various vocal actions, that grant the singer control over all various areas of his complete range, plus the dynamics of the "breath force", from soft to loud, and back to soft. But the most important thing they can do is to create the five so called *"classic Italian vowels".*

The pharyngeal muscles, which to a major degree control the singing vowels, are located in the upper, posterior area of all singer's throat, distant from the muscles of normal speech. They *can only be accessed* by the pharyngeal muscles, but *not by the laryngeal muscles,* which access only the speaking voice's vowels. When the singer successfully accomplishes the development of these pharyngeal, instrumental vowels and sings with them, they give his listeners the illusion that they are hearing the same vowels of normal speech.

The greatest illusion they create, arises from the discrepancy between what the singer must do, muscularly, to produce two-registers-controlled tones, and what he must do muscularly to add the elements of speech, *the instrumental vowels,* to those tones, all of which are accomplished by separate groups of muscles, which are essentially incompatible with each other.

When transforming an inferior vocal condition into a superior one, all changes necessary for improvement are made *primarily* to the *pharyngeal-tract* muscles, *or the head voice,* with the help the instrumental vowels. These pharyngeal muscles are located within the resonating cavities of the *mouth-pharynx* and the *head, and sinus cavities.* With proper development, they effect a permanent change in the muscular responses of the singer's *laryngeal notes, or chest voice tones.*

Proper development of the *pharyngeal tract* can be compared to the developmental methods employed by bodybuilders who hold that, the only way to develop any, and all muscles is through stressing them, by lifting weights, then allowing them to rest. With each successive exercise session, the selected muscles are stressed more strenuously than before, with heavier and heavier weights.

Singers can apply progressively increasing stress to their head voice muscles by "lifting" the inherent, excessive "weight" of the chest voice's muscles, in the manner that body builders use with free, hand-weights. The technique of *lifting the weight of the chest voice* with the falsetto muscle (s) is accomplished by the *messa di voce,* or swelled-tone exercise. In the beginning, the singer can apply *only* as much breath pressure, as the weak detached, starter-falsetto tone can tolerate. After applying stress, the singer must gradually diminish the stress by reducing the volume of the tone back to its starting point, returning the tone to its softest dynamic. Then he must rest his voice.

The ultimate goal of the *swelled-tone exercise* is to increase greater amounts of the chest voice contributions to the selected falsetto starter-tone, until the tone gradually grows to its maximum strength. At that point, the singer should be able to swell the starter tone to the maximum dynamic of *fortissimo,* thereby, completely and safely adding *all* the brilliant, solid *"core sound"* of the chest voice's muscles to the starter-tone.

Success with the *messa di voce* exercise is not available until the original state of the thick, bulky chest voice muscles has been permanently reduced. And, only the full development of the *pharyngeal tract's muscles* can permanently effect this change of the chest voice. So changed, all the chest voice's tones appropriately adjusts themselves in *"weight" and "mass"* and permit the singer the attainment of the five "classic Italian" vowels, in their purest form, plus all five vowels' individual and precise throat-resonator-positions.

In this manner, all the pitches of the tenor's *middle and lower range, from E♮ above middle C, downward to the lowest tone that can be comfortably and musically sung,* and can be produced with the same muscular actions and qualities, as are all the pitches from F♮ above middle C, and upward in the range, to the highest note. When that is possible, all the *chest notes* will have been *"reshaped"* from their original *negative weight and bulky mass* state, and fit into the pre-structured vowel shapes of the upper register's "throat positions."

At that advanced stage of development, the chest voice and head voice's muscular controls are capable of being *"clamped"* to each other (*fiato ferma*), with the aid of the intensified breath stream. With both registers in this harmonious "clamped" state of interaction, all the tones of the singer's complete range, from the lowest to its highest tone, are then under the *protective arc* of the head voice, and the singer can apply, at will, greater or lesser amounts of breath tension to his vocal cords, to satisfy all pitch differences.

Do not allow the words *"breath tension"* to lead you to believe that the intensified breath stream is to be applied with *brute force*. The *"breath force"* should be applied in a firm, but gentle manner, without any *"jerks"* or miscalculations of accurate pitch, and the tone should be stable and be easily and smoothly prolonged and possess a pure, distinct vowel.

The terms *"vowel throat shapes"*, *"resonator shapes and cavities"*, *"hookup points"*, *"clamps"* *"locks"*, *"fiato ferma"*, etc., all come to us from the vocal historical past that produced the art of glorious singing. Here, they have been given updated names, and new twists of applications, but later, references will be made to some of their original names. All of them play critical roles in this *head voice training program* and are helpful and necessary for the cultivation of a superior singing instrument.

Most untrained singers refer to the vowels, solely as those that are utilized when speaking. In many ways, *"spoken vowels"* are similar to the vocal vowels utilized when singing, but in many other ways these spoken sounds are *radically different* from those of the singing instrument. These differences must be clearly understood. The speaking voices' vowels are controlled by the *chest voice*. The "instrumental vowels" are controlled by the muscles of the *head voice*. As the head voice's muscles are undeveloped, with an untrained voice, so are the singer's potential instrumental vowels, and at the start of training, he has no clear image of them, until later on, when proper development reveals them to the him.

CHAPTER FIVE

The *messa di voce exercise*
A brief review of the exercise's history

The *messa di voce* exercise is one of the oldest and most useful tools available to contemporary singers for structuring and maintaining a superior singing instrument. It was created by the master singer-teachers of the *Scuola Cantorum*, a musical conservatory assigned by *Pope Sylvester (314-336 A.D.)*, to fully investigate all technical matters regarding singing and the singing instrument. This investigation ultimately fostered the age of the *castrati, castrated male singers.*

The great value of the *messa di voce* exercise was generally recognized from the time of the *Scuola Cantorum*, and it continued to find favor throughout many subsequent, important vocal training eras. It was greatly relied upon by most teachers of the *Bel Canto* era, and the *"Golden Age of Song"*, which flourished in Italy during the *post-Renaissance* period. During the former period, the art of singing is acknowledged to have achieved its highest degree of perfection.

The exercise remained vitally important throughout the late *17th* and early *18th* centuries, and into the time of such prodigious singer-teachers as *Manual Garcia I* (Père) and his son *Manual Garcia II (Patricio Rodriguez).*

The exercise was also very heavily relied upon during the Paris School's vocal period of the late 18th and early 19th centuries; a *"glamorous" and "colorful"* period dominated by the flamboyant tenor, *Jean de Reszke.* Then the exercise's popularity began to wane and was almost totally discarded in or about the 1950's. Recently, it has not been in use at all, except by *Callas, Sutherland, and Cabballè.*

This seems absurd, since a serious scholar of vocal art may go to any reliable library and find documentation confirming that the *messa di voce* exercise was considered an invaluable training tool by most teachers of the *"great vocal past"*. Why, then, has this exercise been discarded by modern singers and teachers?

Before offering possible explanations for this, it should be understood that by its basic nature, all superior vocal production *must utilize* the basic muscular principles of the *messa di voce. The essential purpose of the exercise is to join together the two separate registers, the head voice and the chest voice, and all its muscular actions and basic timbers, as they are found in all signing voices, male and female.*

When the teachers of singing, throughout the world, decided that the use of the upper *(falsetto)* register was no longer important to vocal structure procedures, that mistake reduced the structuring factor to but to one register: *the chest voice*, with its thick, rebellious, destructive behavior. The mandate of the *messa di voce* exercise is that the singer start a selected pitch with a soft falsetto tone, then gradually and smoothly swell its intensity to a *forte,* with the intention of adding the power of the chest voice to it, then, on the same breath, to then return the tone to the *original pianissimo dynamic.* This feat can hardly be accomplished by most of today's professional singers, with the exception of the lightest and highest coloratura sopranos, and *leggero* tenors, much less by beginning students. The question then arises: in what ways were the great teachers of the historical past able to successfully use the *messa di voce* exercise?

The voice teachers of the *bel canto* period were applying the *messa di voce* exercise exclusively to the voices of the *castrati* singers, castrated men. Because of castration, these "male-sopranos", or *castrati's* vocal mechanisms became permanently altered, denying them the full "natural" muscular growth of the chest voice's muscles. Consequently, their upper *head voice* muscles remained dominant. When the *castrati* performed the *messa di voce* exercise, they did so with *upper register muscles* that were *different* from those of non-castrated men. Therefore, they had an advantage over non-castrated men, and present-day singers.

Because the inherent bulk and power of their chest register muscles were nullified through castration, these *castrati* could facilely *"pull up"* whatever vibrato action of the lower register's muscular controls remained *(after castration),* and achieve a complete joining and collaboration of both the head and chest voice's muscular controls and tonal colors, through the *messa di voce* exercise, thereby transforming the two formerly antagonistic registers into a harmonious "team".

However, when a *non-castrated* young male goes through the physiological changes that occur at puberty, the muscles of his lower *(chest)* register grow in strength and size and gain a natural dominance over the inherently weaker upper *(falsetto)* register muscles. Therefore, when an "unaltered voice" (presumably, all present-day male singers), is assigned the *messa di voce,* the singer is greatly *disadvantaged* and fails.

For contemporary singers to achieve success with the messa di voce exercise, a completely new, contemporary set of rules concerning its application must be applied.

Factors to be aware of when applying the messa di voce exercise

1. The vowel:
>   Proper selection of a particular vowel for a given exercise, and the nature of—
2. The "attack":
>   The correct way of "attacking", or preferably stated—*initiating* any selected tone.
3. Breath tension:
>   The various ways of applying "breath tension", which set the vocal cords into motion, and create vibrations, known as singing tones or pitches, that possess a dynamic range, from soft to loud.
4. How to judge the muscular changes that take place with the progressive development of the singing instrument.
>   a) The physical sensations.
>   b) The sounds that are heard internally, and *only* by the singer himself.
>   c) Properly interpreting what the singer feels and judges about his vocal progress.

EXERCISE NO. 3

Contemporary applications o the messa di voce exercise

The "dramatic" nature of much contemporary vocal literature demands that singers of all vocal categories employ a greater percentage of lower register or "chest voice" participation when singing, than singers of earlier times. As a result, the voices of contemporary singers eventually grow *"larger"* and *"bulkier"* and *"wider"* than singers of the past, and are strongly resistant to the application of the *messa di voce* exercise. This has caused the *messa di voce* exercise to seem totally inapplicable to contemporary vocal training. This misconception can be rectified by presenting some present-day, modified ways in which the exercise can be successfully applied.

Up to this point in the manual, the singer has nowhere been instructed to apply any excessive stress, or to radically increase breath pressure, to any tone produced. However, with the presentation of Exercise # 3, the *messa di voce* exercise, the time has arrived to apply stress, or an *increased amount of*

breath pressure, to certain selected tones, in order to develop their muscular strength.

In the illustrations above, we present several *messa di voce* exercises *which deal with the falsetto tones* of the tenor's upper range, the specific area of the complete range where the purest "starting tone" may be more readily found and accessed. Note that these tones are presented in a descending order, to preserve as much upper register muscular dominance, and purity of tone and vowel as possible. Remember, although these tones are written in the treble clef, they are actually located an octave lower. The singer may select whichever tone that appears most comfortable for him.

The singer should apply the swelled-tone exercise and its principles to such extreme high *falsetto pitches* as high A♮, B♭, B♮, and possibly high C. Even though, as this stage, *total success with these tones is not expected*, whatever *is* accomplished will later help guide the correct structuring of the entire range of chest tones, at the bottom of his range.

Selection of vowels for performing the swelled-tone exercise is related to the structural need of the moment, and each vowel achieves a separate muscular maneuver for the singer. All of the five (5) classic Italian vowels are indispensable; however, each reacts to the exercise in its own way, according to its inherent nature. Below are some *probable impressions* which the singer may get, when applying them to the *messa di voce* exercise, *which from this point onward, will be referred to as the swelled-tone exercise.*

1. The *u (oo) vowel appears* to be "hollow", "wooly", and seems to have no power or its usefulness remains vague. *(Note here, that with the u (oo) vowel, the singer can "erase" or remove any improper chest voice activity of a selected tone , and easily access the breath stream, and both factors are vitally important for the production of all safely produced tones.)*

2. The *i (ee) vowel seems "thin"*, and *"steely"*, has a *"squat"* throat space, and *seems* one dimensional. It demands that the tone be focused to a specific place. (Note here that the singer should not employ the chest voice's i (ee) vowel, since it is highly damaging, but instead he must always use the head voice, or detached falsetto's form of the i (ee) vowel, accompanied by a strong breath flow.)

3. The *e (eh) vowel seems* "thicker" than the i (ee) vowel, yet it is still related to the i (ee), many other ways, which will be explained later.

4. The *o (oh) vowel* immediately seems to demand more throat space and has more "substance" and "weight" than the u (oo), i (ee), e (eh) vowels. (*Note that,* English speaking tenors, with an unconscious reflex-action, try to relate the o (oh) vowel to the a (ah) vowel. However, at this early stage of development the o (oh) vowel should relate more to the u (oo) vowel.)

5. The *falsetto a (ah) vowel* seems to immediately give the singer command of its "placement". (Note here that, the falsetto a (ah) is only safe, when it is made to remain completely detached from any involvement with the "chest voice". And, by comparison to the *falsetto a (ah) vowel*, the *chest voice's a (ah) vowel* is "bulky" and "stiff" and inflexible. It should be the last, of all the vowels tried, for the *messa di voce* exercise.)

These observations are merely mental-imagery conjectures of what a singer may possibly *experience.* However, they may "spark" helpful ideas. All of these mental impressions illustrate why all *guidelines and imagery* presented to a singer, to help him develop his voice, must be clear-cut, focused, and applicable in a specific manner which produces positive results. It is impossible for any singer, reading this manual, hoping to gain some knowledge that could help him improve his voice, to quickly understand what he technically lacks, to successfully perform a given exercise, in the precise manner herein prescribed. Or, conversely what he already possesses, technically, which permits him to successfully perform the exercise. With this in mind, the singer should experiment with the various vowels recommended for these forthcoming swelled-tone exercises. Remembering that, when the breathy u (oo), the hollow o (oh), and the open a (ah)—pronounced like the words hot, pot, lot, not—are applied, *the breath stream is encouraged to flow.* Conversely, when applying the i (ee) and e (eh) vowel, *the breath stream is* <u>*discouraged from flowing.*</u> If a singer experiences a stoppage of the *breath flow* when applying any exercise, then he should stop the exercise and feel free to apply *another vowel* to the exercise instead, mindful of keeping the breath stream flowing, *with all exercises.*

A successful performance of the swelled-tone exercise

Phase #1, The singer establishes a soft G♮ pitch, above middle C *(p. 66),* with a detached falsetto i (ee) vowel, which has been passed through a hollow o (oh) vowel, endeavoring to produce the purest detached, breath-flowing falsetto tone possible. That means, no muscular conflicts with neighboring tones, and no *involvement with chest voice power*. This detached falsetto, starting-tone should convey to the singer a sense of minimal physical effort, because the open i (ee) vowel hones the tone and its breath stream into *a thinly fine, manageable point.* Its tonal quality must be *soft* and *sweet*, and it should possess *no vibrato, or* potential for *projection*. It should be produced in the same "airy" way in which one whistles.

Phase #2, The singer begins to apply breath tension to the detached falsetto, starter-tone, open i (ee) vowel tone, to increase its volume. This requires that, at one point in the swelling process, the singer attempts to "attach" the muscular action of the chest voice to the falsetto starter-tone. To do this, certain structural conditions of the two registers must preexist. The starter-falsetto tone must be developed to a point of sufficient strength to sustain the appropriate breath tension required to *fully pull* the chest voice's muscular power "upward" and "attach" it to the starter-tone. If this advanced development pre-exists, the two registers' separate muscular actions can be connected and "clamped" together on the same pitch by the intensified stream of the breath pressure, and with muscular harmony. If the singer fails to achieve all the aforementioned, then the inherent antagonism between the two registers still exists. If the exercise repeatedly fails, the singer should rest his voice, then try the exercise much later. Perhaps then, using only a breathy u (oo) or a hollow o (oh) vowel. These two vowels restore the free *flow of breath* to the vocal passageway, whereas the i (ee), when *not produced and/or applied accurately,* will cut it completely off.

Eventually, at some point in the swelling process, when the singer attempts to add the "bite" or "core" brilliance of the chest voice to the detached falsetto tone, *a new* and unexpected mechanical function makes itself felt. It is known as the *mezzo-falso,* generally referred as the *"mixed voice" (pg. 79).* While performing the *messa di voce,* the *mixed voice* will help the singer to accomplish a smooth transition from the chest voice to the head voice, and unite the two registers' actions.

This *mezzo-falso is not* an independent mechanical function, but a derivative of both registers' separate muscular actions. It only comes into existence as a result of developing the upper register separately for a long period of time, then coaxing both registers toward a cooperative team effort. When it finally appears, it may be preceded by an unusual, transitory version of its later. permanent self, known as the *"Witch Voice" (p. 77).*

After the muscular controls of the two registers have been clamped together so they do not "crack" apart, they communicate to the singer a precise *"centered point"* along the pharyngeal tract, toward which the breath stream should be focused. This *"clamping" maneuver* can only be accomplished when the breath pressure is first applied directly to the vocal cords, then to its *"focal point"* which guides the singer in locating the center of any tone.

If the singer fails to clamp the two registers' muscular actions firmly together, the vocal cords will *not* be able to sustain the gradual increases and/or decreases of breath tension applied to them, in order to add and/or subtract the power of the chest voice to/or from the starter-falsetto tone. Nor, to precisely raise or lower the pitch. The registers *will "crack apart"* without this "clamping" factor, denying the bonding of the two registers.

When the swelled-tone exercise has been accomplished to ideal standards, the vibrations of any pitch, riding on the breath flow, can then be projected upward, in a posterior direction, along the resonance channel and "soar" toward *their precise terminal impingement points* within the appropriate resonating cavity. *But, only if no separation or blockage exists,* during the *swelled-tone exercise, when passing from the soft, detached falsetto starter tone, to the vibrant power of the chest voice.* With success, harmony comes to exist between the vibrations of the vocal cords, at the bottom of the sound tract, in the lower throat channel, and the sympathetic vibrations of the selected pitch's corresponding resonator cavity, located far above, within the pharynx-mouth-head, or nasal cavities and/or head cavities. Only then can the *"ideal tone"* be produced. Anything other than this above physical "set up" is a compromise and only allows the singer a forced, thick, difficult to manage voice.

The combination of vowels and consonants which accompany a tone, which the singer's listeners recognize as words, are produced by different groups of muscles. The combined muscular actions of the two registers, when successfully used, allow the singer to produce all the vowel sounds that accompany all the pitches with the *head voice muscles*. While the consonants are produced separately by the lips, their surrounding facial muscles, the tongue, and various appropriate positions of the soft palate. These separate groups of muscles must act independently of each other, yet in conjunction with each other. For this to be possible, the singer must possess perfectly "blended registers", managed by the *mixed voice* mechanism. This allows the singer to reduce the power of a selected tone to its minimum, "set" his throat position for the tone's vowel, set the muscles that produce the consonant, then rapidly bring the tone to fulfillment. When this is done correctly, the singer's listeners *cannot* detect that the vowels, consonants, and the pitch are being produced by separate muscular systems.

For the sound waves, produced by the vibrating vocal cords, *far below*, to flow freely *upward* along the *resonance channel*, they must ascend along a vertical, curved pathway, and completely *bypass the forward area of mouth-pharynx cavity*, pass behind the soft and hard palates, and continue traveling upward to the sinus and head resonance cavities. After each tone's sound waves reach their appropriate terminal "hookup" point, located within its appropriate resonator cavity, and *resonate* there, they then travel back down the *sound waves passageway*, exit through the mouth and nasal passageways, and travel outward toward the audience. This all happens very rapidly.

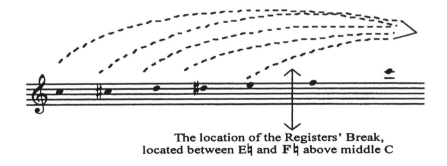

The location of the Registers' Break,
located between E♮ and F♮ above middle C

The pitches of—Middle Range, *C, C♯, D♮, D♯ and E♮*—the five halftones of the tenor's *passaggio,* must be separated from the *chest voice's* muscular control and reassigned to the muscular control of the *head voice—from F♮ to high C*—which represents the tenor's Top Range.

Success with the swelled-tone exercise with the e (eh) vowel indicates an important turning point in structural development

The ultimate goal of the swelled-tone exercise is to unite the two registers' muscular actions and create all five singing vowels u (oo), i (ee), e (eh), o (oh), and a (ah), throughout the singer's complete range. These five vowel, in the order just presented, evoke a range of *throat positions* from "closed" to "open". The u (oo) vowel being the most closed, then moving to the next vowel, the i (ee), which is more open than the u (oo), then to the e (eh), which is more open then the i (ee), and then to the e (eh), the halfway point between a *fully closed throat* position to *a fully open one.* Moving on from the e (eh) to the o (oh), which is more open than the e (eh), and arriving, finally, at the a (ah) vowel, the most *"open throated"* of all five vowels. This range, from close throat position to a fully open throat position, *is not optional*, it is imposed by the unalterable, physiological laws and influences of the vowels. In the earliest phase of training, the u (oo) and i (ee) vowels can be the best vowels to accomplish the swelled-tone exercise, with certain pitches of the range. They u (oo) and the i (ee) inherently closed "head voice" vowels, and most cooperative to the task.

When the singer first achieves a successful swelled-tone exercise with the e (eh) vowel, its "throat position" must be made to lean more toward the open position suggested by the o (oh) vowel, rather than toward the previously developed i (ee) vowel. In that way, the e (eh) vowel will continue developing its throat position toward the o (oh) and a (ah) vowels, still to be accomplished by the swelled-tone exercise. The singer is urged to perform many of the swelled-tone exercises with the newly developed e (eh) vowel. These exercises should start with the tones just above the *passaggio,* from F♮ above middle C, *downward* in the range.

 When success is accomplished the swelled-tone exercise, with the new successful e (eh) vowel, with all the tones of the singer's complete range, the singer can be assured that at least 50% of the chest voice's antagonism toward the head voice has been mollified. The remaining 50% of the chest voice's antagonism will be eliminated when the swelled-tone exercise becomes completely successful with the o (oh) and a (ah) vowels.

An oscillating pattern of exercising the voice

The synergistic nature of the two registers communicates with the singer through *vocal conflicts, and their resolutions.* These *"communications"* must be given full attention, and all conflicts solved. Singers whose voices are dominated by one register, either the bottom register or the top register, don't receive these *"communications"* from their voices, therefore, they have no awareness of the synergistic needs of the *two* registers, since the excluded register offers them few conflicts.

Thus far, we have kept the structuring process focused on exercising the *frequently neglected upper register*. If the singer has had success with the exercises presented so far, then they should have developed the head register to an advantage point wherein it can challenge the chest voice's domination over it. It is then that the singer's voice may communicate to him that *it's time for him to initiate an oscillating pattern of exercising both registers*. This *is not something* which the singer has initiated, but rather, it has been *generated by advanced development of the registers themselves*. From now own, the singer is obliged to follow a *"pendulum-swing pattern"* of exercising his voice; progressively "updating" each register's individual developmental needs, separately from the other register, to keep them both in harmony with each other.

Shifting the structural focus from the head voice toward the chest voice muscles

With the event of a successful performance of the swelled-tone exercise, with the e (eh) vowel and the head voice tones, the singer should then focus his attention on succeeding with the vowels of o (oh) and a (ah). While doing so, it is likely that he will experience a "communication" from his lower register which suggests that he should put his work on the upper register aside and focus his attention on the lower register, for a while. However, when doing so, he should not perform any exercises that challenge nor defeat the singer's progressive success with the swelled tone exercises in the *his upper range.*

Below are several *exercises for the lower range* which and which *do not* challenge nor defeat the progressive success of the swelled-tone exercise with the yet to be "won over" o (oh) and a (ah) vowels.

Above are some exercises *for the lower range area of the voice.* The goal with them is develop the tones indicated in these patterns, but to *not challenge* nor defeat the further development of the upper range's tones. With the *first set,* using the breathy u (oo), the goal is to explore the changes that have occurred with the lower notes, since the growth of upper tones which have begun to *"open up".* With the *second set,* the hollow, open o (oh) vowel is used, and its use automatically adds solidity to the tones. With the *third set,* the singer establishes an open, hollow o (oh) vowel, passes the i (ee) vowel through it, then performs these descending scales. When muscular harmony has been accomplished between the i (ee) vowel and the o (oh) vowel, the new and increased percentage of the chest voice's participation will be revealed to the singer. The singer should then allow his voice a rest period, then do some singing.

The "upward pulling action" of the advanced falsetto voice and the Head Voice Ramp

With each successful performance of the swelled-tone exercise, in a descending direction, while employing the open e (eh) vowel, in a *descending direction,* the singer is creating *another section* of the *"open throated"* vocal tract, which allows the breath stream to flow more freely, from bottom to top of the range.

Relative to the exercises on *page 60*, if the singer experiences *extreme resistance* when attempting to attach the "solid and vibrant" muscular controls of the chest voice to the soft, puffy, aerated, falsetto "starter-tone", *this is not unusual*. There are several ways in which this may manifest itself:

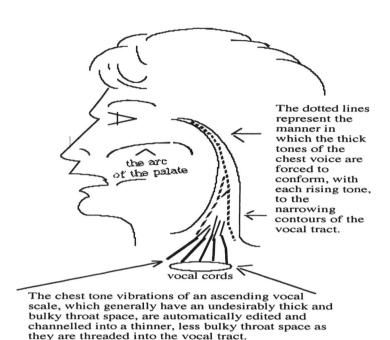

The dotted lines represent the manner in which the thick tones of the chest voice are forced to conform, with each rising tone, to the narrowing contours of the vocal tract.

the arc of the palate

vocal cords

The chest tone vibrations of an ascending vocal scale, which generally have an undesirably thick and bulky throat space, are automatically edited and channelled into a thinner, less bulky throat space as they are threaded into the vocal tract.

1) As the singer's initial attempts to attach chest power to the first *falsetto, starter-tone*, it "pulls away" from the chest power, thereby resisting the coupling process. This could wrongly suggest that the singer is doing something wrong, and that it would be better *not to add* the chest power at all. However, attaching the chest voice to the softer falsetto starter-tone *must be accomplished,* if the ascending scale of the exercises (s) is to be performed. This "pulling away" action of the starter falsetto tone from the starter is a positive sign, which will be explained.

The old master singing teachers, mindful of the difficulties and possible confusion of the student, when first attempting to add the chest voice to the developed head voice, *at the bottom of his range*, after a the long phase of favoring the development of the head voice, urged his pupil to employ the *piccolo martello, (the small hammer),* and to gently *"hammer in"* the power of the chest voice.

The student was instructed to *temporarily bypass the preferred <u>soft</u> approach to the starter-tone* and employ the *piccolo martello,* with a *ff* intensity. The student was instructed to unhesitatingly "lean" or "press" the vibrant quality of the chest voice into the resistant falsetto starter-tone, in a somewhat aggressive manner *(and being mindful that, this was only a temporary approach).* In that way, the falsetto starter-tone would be forced to yield, and to couple with the action of the chest voice. After this approached was mastered, all future attempts at coupling the combined actions of the chest voice to the developed, falsetto tone, with a selected lower range tone, became progressive easier, and the student was advised to return to the more gentle *"bowing" p* breath dynamic approach. When all the tones of an ascending scale harmoniously accept the muscular actions of both registers, the singer has successfully departed from the *"detached head voice mode"*, *and is then using the connect mode of both registers*.

Obviously the "*connected mode*" is the mode used *for performing,*

The aforementioned, *temporary,* more forceful *leaning* into the falsetto starter-tone, to connect the chest voice to it, was termed *appoggiare la voce,* by the past great teachers of the post *Bel Canto* period. In English, this means "to lean" *(the pressure of the breath tension),* directly against the vocal cords.

After the early Italian teachers of *Bel Canto* period established all the fundamental, early rules of vocal structuring, these teachers were succeeded by other great voice teachers of the Neapolitan, Florentine, and Paris schools of vocal training. These later teachers were responsible for establishing new training rules, that applied to singers *other than the castrati:* tenors, baritones and basses; *sopranos, mezzo-sopranos and contraltos,* as we know them today. The Neapolitan, Florentine, and Paris schools of voce training had to prepare their vocal students to cope with *the new, more dramatic and demanding vocal repertory* that had emerged on the scene, after *bel canto* era. This earlier *"dramatic repertory"* gradually progressed to our present-day repertory, which is a mix of dramatic, *versimo,* and *helden (heroic),* with the works of Wagner. But their training principles and applications have been almost totally abandoned by present-day singing teachers.

The great voice teachers of all these earlier periods of vocal training were highly aware of both the *"detached mode"* and the *"connected mode"* of the singing instrument. They were also familiar with the use of the aggressive *martello (little hammer),* sometimes called upon to bring the voice from the *detached mode* into the *connected mode* of the two vocal registers.

Today, the use of the *piccolo martello* is still a valid tool to employ, but *only if* the singer has prepared his voice for it, by first developing the detached falsetto tones of his head voice, for a long time period, then connecting it to the chest voice. Here's the procedure once again: the singer instigates the *appoggio,* or the *"leaning and pressing-in"* of the chest voice's power into the starter-falsetto tone. He applies various amounts of breath pressure *(sometimes strongly, other times gently),* in order to connect the two registers together and generate basic tone, vowel, and precise pitch. After succeeding with the connection process, and while in the *connect mode,* the tone, traveling on the breath flow, must be directed backward and lifted upward, posteriorly in the throat, back of the soft and hard palates, sending the tone along with the breath stream, sailing smoothly along the ascending vertical pathway of the vocal tract, to the it's appropriate resonator-cavity.

One of the noteworthy responses of the advanced development of the *detached falsetto* is that, it often aggressively resists being connected to the power of the chest voice in an usual manner, by "flying" away from it, and upwards towards the top of the singer's range. This behavior, which seems totally negative, when use properly, can be greatly beneficial to the singer, since it assists him with all ascending vocal movement, when he succeeds in connecting the "run-away, falsetto starter tone, to the chest voice's power." Afterward, and initiating an ascending scale, he must not attempt to "ground or anchor" the tone to a specific spot, but instead, allow the "upward-pulling factor" to pull the starter tone upward and backward in the throat, along the curved, vertically ascending resonance channel. This gliding, upward-pulling factor gives all exercise scales, and vocal phrases their professional sounding *"ease"* and superior, highly musical qualities.

This superior vocal method of singing up or down the vocal resonance channel is the *direct opposite* of the incorrect *pushing-up* maneuvers used by the majority of present-day singers. Most of them generally operate on *a false principle* that "the tone (s) must be "pushed" upward, with a strong driving force. The *upward pulling, positive action,* generated by the advanced development of the falsetto and the falsetto i (ee) vowel, can be compared to the wound-up spring of a clock. Or, the smooth-gliding movement of an escalator. It first reveals itself to the singer-student, at a point in the development of his falsetto range, when he first senses that it is now time to connect the two registers separate and antagonistic actions together. We have already explained the correct methods of connecting the two registers above, so please review it.

The exercises of Figure #1 (*next page*) are used to correctly structure the *passage tones—middle-C, C#, D♮, D#, and E♮*. Note that they start above the *passaggio*, and their pattern of development must be in a *descending direction*. This assures that they are being controlled by the muscles of the *head voice*, from F♮ above middle C, as opposed to being controlled by the chest voice's muscles, from B♮ below middle C, downward to the bottom of the range. At first, the singer should *only employ* the breathy falsetto u (oo) vowel, and the hollow o (oh) vowel to them, accompanied by a prolonged, free flow of breath. A new breath must be taken for each succeeding exercise.

The hollow u (oo) and o (oh) vowels assure the singer that there is no negative, thickness or weightiness of the chest voice, influencing them. He should perform all the scales of Exercise #1, several times a day, but with rest periods of an half hour or hour, between sessions. Afterward, he must allow the voice to rest for a day or two, then applied them again. Then he should use similar descending scales, with the same u (oo) and o (oh) vowels, in other parts of his range, using his judgment in deciding where, precisely, they seem most appropriate. But, for a while, both the i (ee) and e (eh) vowels *should not be employed*, because *they tend to stop the breath flow,* and establishing the free flow of breath is one of the chief benefit of these exercises.

Special exercises for structuring the Passaggio tones

#1

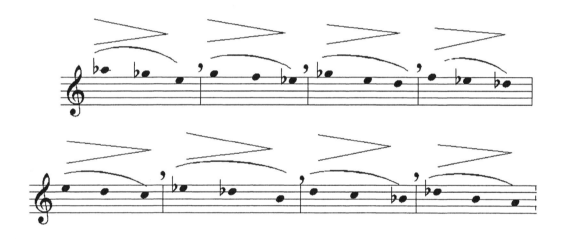

Training the tongue and soft palate to assume their proper the positions and their behavior movements

The soft palate should be lowered, not raised, as is generally believed, and moved downward and forward, in the direction of the mouth cavity. And the tongue must be repositioned upward from the lower throat channel, and placed into the mouth cavity. Accomplishing both the factors clears a passageway for the breath flow to flow through all the tones of the *passaggio*. The breath flow, an intensified, concentrated stream of air, emanating from the lungs, must have a free and fluid passageway from the bottom of the range, through the *passage tones,* located in the upper posterior area of the mouth-pharynx cavity, then 'whiz' further upward, into the resonating cavities of the sinus and skull. If both the soft palate and the tongue are not positioned as instructed above, then the *"wide passaggio"*, from B♭ below middle C to the G♮ above it, will remain totally blocked and deny the breath flow from passing through the *"wide passaggio"*, thus, fragmenting the complete vocal range in its upper middle, and making the all its tones dysfunctional, and compromised, with regard to precise intonation and pure vowels.

Retraining the tongue's basic movements and positions, so it can perform its duties of shifting from vowel to vowel *(posteriorly, in the back of the throat)* and aiding in the creation of the consonants, which are achieved frontally with the lips, in collaboration with the upper movements of cheeks, can be achieved in the following manner.

In the illustration below, while the pitches are the same as *Exercise #1*, they must be exercised in a different manner, as now explained:

#2

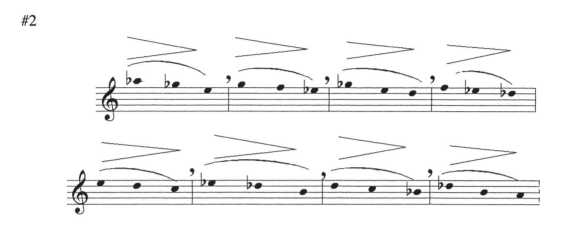

The tongue and *soft palate* can both be trained, or more accurately *retrained,* as to their correct positions and movements, while singing, by performing a series of descending scales. Establish a *very soft*, detached falsetto, fully opened-throated a (ah) vowel, with the top note of each new measure, then slowly change it to a detached falsetto, fully opened throated i (ee), while a strong breath stream blows through the tone. The singer should note that the just before starting to change the first open a (ah) vowel to the open throated, detached falsetto i (ee) vowel, the i (ee) vowel, the singer must lift his tongue out of his lower throat channel and move it upward and into his mouth cavity.

After the tongue has been *repositioned* inside the mouth cavity, its mid-section should hunch upward into a mound, and imitate the shape of the hard palate, located just above it. Meanwhile, the tip of the tongue must be moved forward in the mouth cavity, toward the front teeth. Make sure that a good flow of breath accompanies the open i (ee) vowel, attained through this exercise.

The singer may perform these exercises many times during the day, *but with periods of rest, in between them.* Then he should completely rest his singing voice for a day or two. When he returns to his exercise period, he should perform all the exercises of *group #3. The 3rd group of exercises (below),* employing *the swelled-tone exercise*, with the AW vowel sound.

The *AW* is not a pure, Classic Italian vowel, but rather a combination of the u (oo), o (oh), and a (ah) vowels. It can be most helpful in gradually bringing the tones of *E♭, E♮, F♮ and G♭* to an important advanced state of development, which is to remove all of them from the muscular controls of the chest voice, then attach them to the muscular controls of the head voice, from F♮ above middle to the B♮ above, and into a new state, wherein the both registers muscular contributions or active, but with the head voice muscles, in possession of the dominant control. From then on, the advanced falsetto's muscular controls from F♮ to B♮ above middle C become their new, permanent "owner".

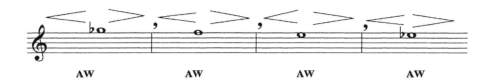

The above exercises respond more readily *when they are performed in a descending direction.* This gives the singer a huge advantage in establishing their correct throat positions, since the first pitch of the exercise, G♭ above middle C, is *"safely"* located within the boundaries of head voice register.

The *AW* vowel sound can be most accurately "pronounced" and positioned in the singer's upper, posterior throat area, when it is modeled after the English words: *bought, sought, caught, taught, and hawk.* The reason that the AW is so helpful for transferring the muscular controls of these *critical passage tones, E♭, E♮, F♮, and F♯ is* because, when performing ascending vocal exercises, and arriving at arriving at the E♭ above middle-C, the singer must make a *"switch"* from the chest register's muscular controls, completely over to the muscular controls of head register.

If your throat and tongue respond unfavorably to all these above exercises, stop performing them and rest your voice for a good while. Upon returning to these exercises eliminate the *setting of the open-throated a (ah) vowel's position, and the i (ee) vowel* completely, and use only the u (oo), o (oh), and AW vowels for all phases of these exercises, sometimes together, and other times individually.

Advancing the development of the "cross-over" tone of E♭ above middle C

This may be accomplished by performing a series of *swell and diminish exercises* with the tones of *Group 3,* adding a new "twist", using both the detached falsetto i (ee) and e (eh) vowels. The new manner of performing *Group 3's* exercises is to establish a detached falsetto i (ee) vowel with the top pitch of the first measure *(see the illustration above),* which is a G♭ above the registers' break, and slowly start swelling it. As soon as the i (ee) vowel has been swelled to an *f dynamic,* slowly change the i (ee) to the more open-throated position of the e (eh) vowel. After the e (eh) vowel has been accomplished and its new throat position stabilized, start swelling the tone to an *fff dynamic,* then attempt to diminish the tone complete back to a *ppp dynamic.* Rest the voice for an half hour, then do the same exercise again, with the pitches of the second, third and fourth measures.

After a period of time, repeat all these exercises from their beginning, but *this time,* after the detached falsetto tone with the i (ee) vowel has been established and has stabilized, swell the tone to a *f dynamic, then gradually* change the i (ee) throat socket to a fully open-throated a (ah) vowel, then swell the tone toward an *fff dynamic,* then diminish it back to the soft intensity of *p.* Then rest your voice again. After a good period of time, sing some simple songs *(preferable one of the Italian Classic songs),* and observe what effect these exercises has had upon your singing voice *(p. 87). Rest your voice for a good while, Then perform a soft passage through the u (oo), to the o (oo) and the AW vowels, on a single sustained pitch.*

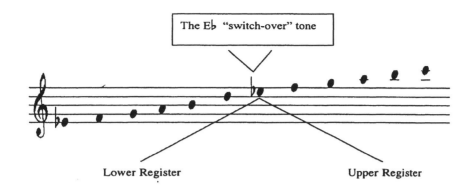

If you think of the E♭ above middle C as *a fulcrum point,* located in the center of your complete range, between your chest voice's lower tones and your head voice's upper tones, you may get some insight into why the *middle range* acts as a fulcrum.

Here is an excellent dictionary definition of the word: *fulcrum, an agent through which vital powers are passed through.* In the case of the *E♭ "switch-over" tone,* situated above middle C, managing the power of the breath pressure while ascending the range and arriving at the E♭, *and gradually* readying it to switch the muscular controls from the chest muscles, and completely over to the head muscles, is the main difficulty. This is how that is successfully done—as an *ascending* exercise scale or vocal phrase approaches the E♭, *(while using the u (oo), o (oh), or AW vowel), you* must reduce the volume of one of two half pitches, immediately below the E♭, (D♮ and/or D♭), rendering them *"hollow" and "somewhat breathy",* then gradually switch the control of the tone from the chest muscles to the head muscles on the E♭ *"cross-over tone",* then immediately swell its volume. Doing this transfers the power from the chest register to the head register, and it establishes the tone's precise throat position, which is rather unusual, but it clarifies for the singer why these *"illusive" passaggio tones* are seldom properly trained. The *head voice muscles must forever exert complete control of the E♭, E♮, F♮, and F♯ tones,* above middle C, as well as all the tones above F♯, and further upward to the top of the range.

The next factor to consider in solving the problem of the E♭ above middle C's "switch over" tone is *which of the five vowel* is best to apply to it. The answer is that—before performing any exercise which is meant to strengthen these above mentioned pitches, the singer should perform many preparatory, descending falsetto exercises, in order to infuses these tones with generous amounts of breath flow. The u (oo), o (oh), or the AW vowel is best for accomplishing this. If we could dissect the AW vowel sound, we would understand that it is made up of the u (oo), open o (oh) and open (ah) vowels—which are *the three airflow, enabling vowels.* This combination of vowels is highly advantageous for the singer because, with all the *passaggio* tones, and in particular the E♭ "switch over" tone, the AW possesses all the muscular-controls which can help him to convert the E♭ above middle C, from a chest voice dominated tone, to a totally head voice dominated tone.

These are the maneuvers that should be performed to accomplish this task:

The singer establishes the detached falsetto, E♭, situated above middle C pitch, with the u (oo) vowel component of the AW sound, and as softly as possible. Then, he begins to apply the breath stream while slowly repositioning the E♭ tone further upward and backward in his throat, and away from the lower register's control. While doing so, and in order to precisely "place the E♭ he should now position his throat toward an open i (ee) vowel. When that's been accomplished, he must guide the E♭ his throat's position toward a bright, fully open i (ee) vowel, then swell it to an *f dynamic,* simultaneoulsy lifting the pitch as far away from the muscular control of the chest voice as is possible. At that point, a total transfer of the E♭ has been accomplished, but only with the i (ee) vowel.

> In an interview, held by *Martine Kettle*, in *The Guardian,* with the great soprano, *Dame Joan Sutherland*, Joan told him:
> "The old manuals were right, Garcia, Lamperti, the others. People don't learn to breathe, support and project. And they don't sing vocalise. There are great volumes of exercises that give you the legato line and help you join the *middle voice* to the *upper voice.* But now they sing down here . . .
> ("in the throat", *author's explanation*), and then they stab at the top. They don't know how to get there properly, and they will pay the price in the end."
> Dame Joan Sutherland
> The Guardian - May 8, 2002

Possessing skill in managing the four "switch-over" tones, *E♭, E♮, F♮ and F♯,* above middle C, while actually singing, is in truth a most difficult task and a "rare art", seldom accomplished these days. However *possessing or not possessing that skill* precisely defines what having a "superior talent for singing" really means.

The transportable chest voice power

The phrase, *"transportable chest voice power",* actually refers to the vibrations of the vocal cords, and not the chest register, itself. When the vocal cords' vibrations are *"blocked"* at the bottom the singer's range, and unable to travel upward, along the resonance channel, due to the negative, unblended chest voice's muscular controls, which deprives them from being "mixed" with the breath flow, they remain trapped within the lower section of the range. But, once these "trapped" vocal cords vibrations have been mixed with the breath stream, they become kinetic, and are free to flow out of the lower chamber and ascend the range towards one of the resonance cavities, either the *mouth-pharynx cavity*, the sinus cavities, or the cavities of the skull and reach the singer's desired pitch .

However, it must be understood that "the full length *(or passageway),* of the entire resonance channel is not *"arranged"* in a strait, vertically ascending line. Instead, it follows a *curved ascending line of ascent*, through the windpipe, the *mouth-pharynx cavity*, and finally the very tiny passageways of *the nasal* and *head cavities.*

Therefore, the singer must envision the resonance channel as a vertically *curved,* ascending pathway, along which he must sing the notes of his assigned musical pieces, by directing the selected pitch's breath stream toward its appropriate resonance cavity. And, he must know that *the breath stream , does not automatically flow* into any of these critically important resonance cavities, but that *it is he* who must direct the breath stream, upward along the resonance channel and towards the desired pitch's *focal point.* This *pitch and its focal point* may be located in either the mouth-pharynx, or the *sinus cavities,* or the *head cavities,* which greatly influence the tone's quality, accuracy and successful fulfillment.

In order to locate a selected tone's focal point, within any of the above mentioned resonance cavities, the singer must consciously lift his larynx upward towards the upper, posterior area of his throat, in order for him to direct the energized breath stream behind his soft palate, to access the proper pathway of the particular resonance cavity which is appropriate for the presently sung tone.

The detached, falsetto i (ee) vowel, when combined with any softly sung pitch above the registers' break *(from F♮ above middle C, to the very top of the tenor's range),* when it is swelled, will move the soft palate correctly downward and forward, in the direction of the entrance to the mouth cavity. The specific focal point of any and all of the pitches from Fn above middle C to the top of the range, are located along the arch of the hard palate. It is toward these individual and precise *focal points that line the hard palate,* readily identified by the detached falsetto i (ee) vowel, then developed to its fullest, by swelling the detached falsetto i (ee) vowel, towards which the singer must direct the highly energized breath stream. However, locating these individual *"focal points"* can not be accomplished if the soft palate has not first been lowered and repositioned forward, toward the entrance into the mouth cavity, as directed above.

When the breath stream arrives at the precise focal point of any selected pitch, the energized breath stream, which tends to be unstable, will become stationary and attached itself to a specific spot, which is that particular pitch's focal point, and the singer will the feel that specific spot clearly and acutely. Therefore, he know, precisely, where to direct the power of the breath stream, and enable the vibrations of the vocal cords to fulfill that particular pitch.

When the appropriate *focal point* is *first* located, the sound quality of that specific pitch will be *"dull" and "muted",* since it is in an undeveloped state. Carefully developing the tone, through judicious applications of the swell and diminish exercise, using the detached falsetto i (ee) vowel, will eventually allow the vibrato action of the vocal cords to pierce the initial opaque quality of the selected tone, whereupon the "resonance factor" of the tone will immediately "lights it up", with sparking brilliance, projecting the tone's new, bright sounds outward towards the singer's listener (s). As time passes and the singer reputedly locates this same pitch's focal point, and applies the swell and diminish exercise it, the selected pitch's focal point will grow in strength and allow the singer to attached the *full power of the chest voice* to its, and with all five individual, classical Italian vowels. However, each individual vowel takes a different amount of time to achieve its total development, with that same particular pitch's focal point.

This operation then reveals to the singer the basic nature of the *vibrato action* of the vocal cords, and he will understand that it is a highly mobile action, due to inherent kinetic nature of the breath force, and its swirling currents. These vibrations can never be permanently restricted to any particular focal point, otherwise the singer would only be able to sing just one particular pitch, over and over. The breath force, which controls the attainment of any selected pitch, must be retained in a highly mobile state, ready and waiting for the in singer to send it traveling, toward the next desired pitch that is to be sung. It is because of these above factors, concerning the combined vibrato action and the highly mobile nature of the breath force that I have given their maneuvers the name of *"The transportable power of the chest voice".*

Many successful singers express how they accomplish the above maneuvers by stating: "I can adjust, then clamp my larynx to my soft palate, with any particular note of my complete range, then send the breath force and the vibrations of the vocal cords toward the particular pitch's focal point, and then, I keep supplying the tone with breath and allow vocal cords to sing the tone for me.

Properly clamping the larynx together, with its proper *"focal point",* with various selected pitches, along the length of the resonance channel, also reveals to the singer the small aperture (*or hole*), of each individual pitch of the complete range, through which, the energized breath stream, and the vibrations of the vocal cords, must pass through, to accomplish the sired pitch of the moment.

None of the above could be physiologically possible, unless the head voice's muscular controls, especially when using the correct i (ee) vowel, didn't enable the singer to move his soft palate forward and downward toward the front of the mouth, free his larynx from its low resting position, then raise it upward toward a specific resonance cavity, and connect it to the specific pitch's *focal point*, of the pitch that he wishes to sing. The contributions of the specific resonance cavity where the selected pitch is located then amplifies the tone, and enhances its timbres. Success with all these maneuvers requires that *the larynx not be anchored at some inappropriate position*, in the lower throat channel, *but instead be poised and waiting, in an extremely flexible and mobile state,* ready to move, at a moment's notice, so that the singer can quickly lift it out of its resting place and direct it toward a specific pitch, located within a specific resonance cavity. This adjusting and tuning of the larynx's various position must be consciously and physically controlled by the singer, and no amount of dreaming, or aesthetic posturing will do the task for him, instead!

Ascending vocal movement

All ascending vocal movement has an injurious potential for the singing instrument, if the correct structuring of the head voice tract has not been accomplished. A completely and accurately structured vocal tract, with a free passageway from it lowest to its highest tones, allows the *breath force* to flow rapidly up and down, within it. It also allows the singer's to produce all the tones of his complete range *as if* they were controlled by *one muscular system*, whereas, in reality, they are being controlled and manipulated by various groups of muscles, that must interact harmoniously with each other. When the resonance tract is correctly and completely structured, all the tones of the singers range give his listeners the impression that the singer possesses but a single, harmonious method of tone production, with each tone matching the other in quality and muscular action, and all possessing varied, beautiful, interesting timbres.

In terms of *quality of sound*, the master-teachers of the past labeled a superior voice's ideal tonal color *chiaro scuro*. Translated from the Italian, *chiaroscuro* means *clear and dark*. In muscular terms, when a singer's voice possesses *chiaroscuro,* each and every tone of his range complete range possesses a perfectly-proportioned percentage of the two register's *best tonal qualities and muscular actions* : the inherent *"brightness"* of the *chest voice*, without its negative factors of bulk and thickness, and the *"somber colors"* of the *head voice*, without its earlier limitations, of not possessing projecting power and tonal brilliance.

To become *a professional singer*, all singers are obliged to maintain their voices in a superior, performance condition. Therefore, it is critical that the singer observe several important factors:

1) "The upward pulls", created by the advanced *"detached falsetto"* utilizing the *detached falsetto mode of the i (ee) vowel*, must aide and guide each and every tone of an ascending phrase to rise toward the *top of the range*, as opposed to pull the scale downward, toward the *bottom of his range*.

2) The inherent *"bulk"* or *"mass"* of the chest voice's negative influence must be continuously restrained, as the scale rises higher and higher in the range. This can only be repeatedly accomplished, when the singer makes a conscious effort to "thread" each individual higher pitch of the rising scale toward the small aperture of the selected pitch, in order for the breath flow to enter into it, as opposed to the singer attempting to inappropriately widen his throat position, with each successive higher pitch.

3) As an ascending scale approaches the span of the *"wide passaggio"*, B♭ below middle C, up to F♮ and F♯ above middle C, *the singer must transfer the "work load" of each successive ascending tone within the passaggio, away from the chest voice's muscular controls, and over to the muscular controls of the head voice.* Assuring that from E♭ above middle C, and including the *E♮, F♮ and F♯* located above it, are also transferred completely over to the controls of the upper, head voice register.

With the forthcoming exercises of *Figures 1 and 2 (below)*, the widely-spaced intervals between the notes of each exercise, force the singer to utilize the principles of the *swelled-tone* exercise to accomplish them correctly. When ascending from one note to the next, the singer starts a selected tone softly, swells it, then softens it again, in order to initiate the ascending movement toward the next, higher note. Then, upon securing it, the singer increases the breath tension again. Applying breath tension in this above manner helps the singer to avoid dragging up the negative factors of the chest voice from the first note, to the second note. It is nearly impossible for the singer to perform a widely-spaced interval *(in a smooth, musical fashion),* without calling upon the principles of the *swelled-tone exercise.* The widely-spaced intervals of each exercise also help the singer to discover two important factors about ascending his vocal range:

A) The correct method of "shifting" from the vowel throat-socket of the first pitch to the vowel throat-socket of the upper, second pitch.

B) The correct method of withholding power or core brilliance, by altering the level of the breath intensity, so that "power" may only be brought into play, at the singer's discretion, through swelling or diminishing the tone.

Figure 1

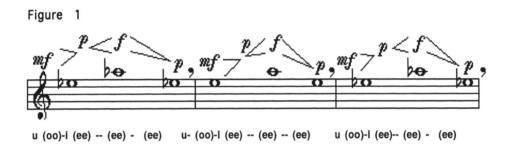

u (oo)-i (ee) -- (ee) - (ee)   u- (oo)-i (ee) -- (ee) -- (ee)   u (oo)-i (ee)-- (ee) - (ee)

Figure 2

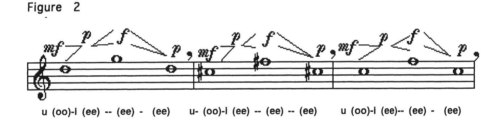

u (oo)-i (ee) -- (ee) - (ee)   u- (oo)-i (ee) -- (ee) -- (ee)   u (oo)-i (ee)-- (ee) - (ee)

Figures 1 and 2 (above) present the singer's with his first *ascending scales.* Note that they are widely-spaced. This factor restricts the singer from "*dragging up*" excessive chest voice "weight". The *i (ee) vowel* should be used, after passing it through an u (oo) vowel, to assure that it has been placed in its *head voice mode,* meaning *no connection to the power of the chest voice until the singer decides its appropriate to do so.* Achieving those factors is completely dependent upon a free flow of the breath force. The correct i (ee) vowel guides the singer in *narrowing and focusing* the first, highly-energized tone of the pattern upward and backward in the throat, and behind the soft and hard palates.

For tenor voices, in particular, the performance of ascending vocal phrases and/or exercise is a more critical matter than for singers of other vocal categories. The tenor's early training period must be focused almost exclusively upon establishing a complete dominance of the head voice's muscles of their upper tones, specially with the tones of the *passaggio,* resulting in a vocal condition wherein his voice may temporarily feel and sound totally falsetto dominated.

Reviewing the history of some of the greatest tenors of history: *Caruso, Gigli, Bjöerling, McCormack, Lauri-Volpi, Schipa* and the young *Di Stefano,* one finds evidence that the timbres and muscular actions of *their earlier vocal efforts* were dominated by the *"lyric quality"* of upper register's sound. As their vocal development progressed, they gradually added more of the activities of the *chest voice* to all of their tones, which permanently altered their voices in physical character, sound, and usage. And also, it influenced their selection of the operatic roles, which they wished to sing. All these great tenors were considered to have achieved the near perfect vocal state of *"pure" or "true" tenor voice*, meaning they sang with bright, lyric, and powerful tenor sounds, not the sounds of the baritone voice. Admittedly, Caruso's later recording reveal him singing with darker, baritonal qualities.

The "Bari-Tenors" of recent times

A decade or three ago, several outstanding tenors of international fame appeared on the vocal scene whose voices *were not structured* to the advanced level and standards of a *"pure and true tenor"*, as were the voices of most tenors of the past, mentioned on the previous page. Compared to them, these more recent tenors were, in a sense, "baritone-tenors". This suggests that their vocal training and structuring must have been vastly different, in some way, than tenors of the past, and that is was less than complete. Consequently, their voices had remained in a compromised and unfulfilled vocal state— *somewhere between baritone and tenor.* Each of these modern-day tenors possessed great voices and were, no doubt, sincere and dedicated artists. Nevertheless, they performed with many vocal limitations, such as *impure vowels* and *thickness of tone,* especially in the "passaggio" area. They often sang with sluggishness of vocal movement, produced boring, monochromatic tones, and often with unclear and "strange vocal diction."

Figure 3

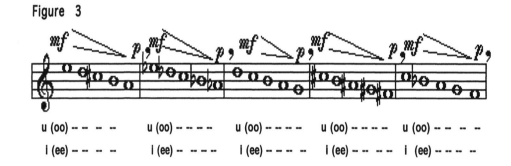

u (oo) -- -- -- --   u (oo) -- -- -- --   u (oo) -- -- -- --   u (oo) -- -- -- --   u (oo) -- -- -- --

i (ee) -- -- -- --   i (ee) -- -- -- --   i (ee) -- -- -- --   i (ee) -- -- -- --   i (ee) -- -- -- --

Figure 4

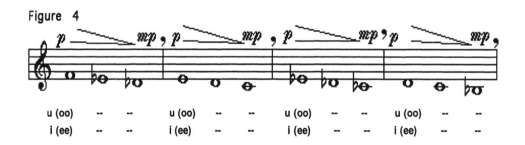

u (oo) -- --   u (oo) -- --   u (oo) -- --   u (oo) -- --

i (ee) -- --   i (ee) -- --   i (ee) -- --   i (ee) -- --

Surely, the limitations of these *"Bari-tenors"* were caused by the negative aspects of their chest voice. We assume that these *"baritone-tenors" did not* have at their disposal sufficient, knowledge of how to develop their voices to a "purer" state of tenor singing. Perhaps then, they would have become *"pure tenors"*, like most of the great tenors of the past. If any present-day student-tenor, reading what has just been presented above, feels that his own voice is that of a "Bari-tenor", and he wants to apply exercises to his voice that will help him to become a "pure tenor", he may start structuring his voice toward a state of "pure and true tenor", by first applying some of the exercises below. With *Figures 3 and 4 (below),* we have a series of descending preparatory scales that should be executed, before passing on to the *exercises of 5 & 6,* which are to be performed with the *detached falsetto u (oo) vowel,* then with *the i (ee) vowel.* They should be performed for quite a long time before passing on to the ascending scales of *Figures 5, 6 & 7 (below).*

Figure 5

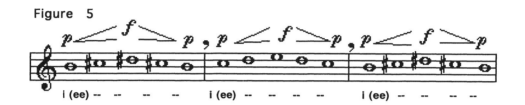

With figure 5, note that in *measures 1 & 3,* the addition of the first note of B♮ below the middle C unavoidably adds more "chest weight" to the pitches of to the *D♭, D♮, E♭ and E♮* above middle C. It may be helpful, in between performances of the exercises of 5 & 6, to rest the voice for a few hours, or a day, return to the exercises of figures 3 & 4, rest the voice again, and on then return to the *exercises of 5 & 6.* It may also be helpful and rather instructive to perform a few single, sustain tones with the pitches of middle *C, D♭, D♮, E♭ and E♮* above middle C, starting with an i (ee) vowel, then gradually and smoothly passing to a fully open a (ah) vowel, but without taking a new breath in-between the two vowels.

Figure 6

Figure 7

Getting ready to sing after vocalization

After exercising the voice for a reasonable length of time, the singer should rest his voice for a long period of time, to allow the muscles of his vocal instrument to readjust to the influences of the exercises. After the voice feels rested, then do some singing. This is the most reliable way to evaluate progress. Some of the most beneficial pieces to sing are the *Italian Songs and Arias of the Seventeenth and Eighteenth Century.* They can easily be found in a single collection at any reputable music store. I have made a list of those I recommend most often, and have divided them into two main categories

The classic songs and arias of the Seventeenth and Eighteenth Centuries

Some of the most charming and vocally beneficial performance pieces are the *24 Italian Songs and Arias of the Seventeenth and Eighteenth Century.* They are divided into two groups; those with *slow, sustained movement*, and those with *fast vocal movement.* Singers whose voices are trained in a manner that includes the muscular actions and qualities of both vocal registers find these songs highly beneficial to the development and discovery of their singing voices, and a delight to perform. Singers who rely exclusively on the *chest voice, ascending-scales-method* of voice training, which produces thick tones and a limited control of dynamics, generally find them "difficult", "boring", and "useless". Of course, their negative attitude toward these masterpieces is understandable, since an incorrect vocal technique forbids one to perform them properly.

The composers who wrote these songs and arias were, in most cases, master singers and master-voice-teachers themselves. The dynamic markings and interpretative expressions inscribed throughout these vocal masterpieces are usually in perfect harmony with the correct physiological laws of the well trained singing instrument. When duly observed, these markings give the singer a most helpful guide for achieving a healthy, consistently well-functioning and superior vocal instrument.

Group 1: The Sustained Pieces:

1. *Amarilli, mia bella*	G. Caccini
2. *Comme raggio di sol*	A. Caldara
3. *Sebben, crudele*	A. Caldara
4. *Vergin, tutto amor*	F. Durante
5. *Caro mio ben*	G. Giordani
6. *O del mio dolce ardor*	C. W. Von Gluck
7. *O cessate di piagarmi*	A. Scarlatti
8. *Tu lo sai*	G. Torelli

Group 2: The Flexible Pieces:

9. *Per la gloria d'adorarvi*	G. Bononcini
10. *Che fiero costume*	G. Legrenzi
11. *Pur dicesti, o bocca bella*	A. Lotti
12. *Il mio bel foco*	B. Marcello
13. *Nel cor più non mi sento*	G. Paisiello
14. *Se tu m'ami, se sospiri*	G. Pergolesi
15. *Già il sole dal Gange*	A. Scarlatti
16. *Le Violette*	A. Scarlatti
17. *Se Florindo è fedele*	A. Scarlatti

Understand that the songs from *Group 1*, with their *sustained* phrases, inherently add a greater percentage of chest voice participation to the singing voice than do the *fast-moving* songs of *Group 2*, with their flexible vocal movement. The *sustained songs* also "gather" all tones of the complete range, especially those of the *passaggio,* into a close interrelationship, revealing to the singer how advanced is his *legato* movement.

The fast moving songs of *Group 2* allow the head voice *(or more accurately, the mixed voice)* to dominate every phrase. They create a *benign, beneficial separation* between tones and somewhat restrict legato action. This is because it is difficult to apply maximum breath tension to any tone or phrase when it is "flying by" at a rapid tempo.

It is desirable for the average beginner to make a careful study of the manner in which all his tones are being produced. It is therefore more practical for the first songs of any "singing session" to be chosen from the slow, sustained pieces of *Group 1.* These allow the beginner to closely scrutinize all technical matters.

Singers *cannot* hear the quality of their voices as others do. And, the physical act of singing often seduces the singer into a euphoric state of self-satisfaction in which judgments of his vocal standards may be distorted. Therefore, it is beneficial and practical for singers to periodically ask their teachers, vocal coaches, or someone whose judgment they trust, to tell them if the tones which they are producing possess beauty, and/or if they are of a potentially professional standard. It is possible for a singer to produce tones *that seem* to be correct and beautiful but which are, *in reality,* unpleasant to hear. It is up to those asked to judge the singer's vocal tones to tell him the truth, as they perceive it.

The nature and important function of the impingement or "hookup" points that line the vocal tract

When we consider the *breath pressure* or "motor force" necessary for singing, when it is applied to any given tone, in order to develop its strength, and to achieve precise intonation, the intention is to stress it. For the singer to become familiar with the precise location of any particular *focal* or *hookup point* for the breath force, the tone selected for exercise must be started with the purest and softest possible volume a breathy *u (oo) or hollow o (oh) vowel.* Both vowels encourage a free flow of breath. Next, the singer changes either the breathy u (oo) or the hollow o (oh), into an open *detached falsetto* i (ee) vowel. This particular mode of the i (ee) vowel allows the singer to move his larynx from its resting position toward the selected tone's focal point. This is primarily, but not completely, accomplished by mental imagery, guiding the upward pulling muscles which are controlled by the falsetto i (ee) vowel, when it is totally free from any and all attachments to the or chest voice muscles, and it is "gliding" and being pulled upward, toward the top of the range, by the head voice muscles. While the singer is accomplishing the lifting of his larynx, his lips and cheeks make important movements, too. His cheeks slowly to rise upward toward his eyes, and his lips "curl" upward at their ends, in a semi-smile. After positioning the both larynx and pharynx close up, against each other, and clamps them fast to each other, the singer begins to apply the thin, highly energized steam of breath pressure to the precise throat position, the presently sung pitch, indicated to him by the falsetto i (ee) vowel's position.

There exists a potential for the tone to stray from its precise *focal point,* where the i (ee) vowel had placed it, and to distort and thicken toward the wider e (eh) vowel . If this should happen, the singer must stop the tone and start another tone, in the same manner as he did with the first tone.

Initially, the selected tone can *only sustain minimal breath pressure*, without immediately straying from its precise i (ee) vowel, focal point position *(the "center of the bull's eyes"),* and distorting its vowel. This becomes very discouraging for the student-singer who seldom has a realistic concept of how long and arduously the task of completely developing any selected tone's focal point may actually take. Especially with the difficult tones of his *"wide passaggio area"* — B♭ below middle C, to the F♮ and F♯ above middle C, since they take longer than all other tones, of the complete vocal range, to yield to total development. The student may be comforted by the fact that, when any given tone has been developed to its fullest, all its benefits of precise intonation, regulation of exact proportions of chest and/or head voice, superior tone quality, and potential agility, are all fully granted to him. Thereafter, the technique of acquiring all these assests are not so easily lost of forgotten, since they were acquired very slowly, over what seemed like an endless period of time.

When the *focal points* of every tone in the singer's range have all been completely developed, they automatically *"invite"* the lower register to join the head voice muscles, at the specific rendezvous point of each of their focal points and operate together, as a team effort, and possess a potential for superior singing. Each focal point, from middle C upward, to the highest possible tone, possesses its own unique character and timbre, and reacts differently to each of the five vowels, *u (oo), i (ee), e (eh), o (oh) and a (ah)*. The same is true of all the tones from middle C, downward, as far as possible, but they can only be truly understood, *after* all the top tones have been fully developed.

The singer should start a selected tone with an breathy u (oo) vowel, or a hollow o (oh) vowel, and slowly change it to a detached falsetto, open i (ee) vowel, allowing for the tongue's repositioning movements; the tongue moves upward out of the lower throat channel, enters into the mouth-pharynx cavity, hunches itself upward in the shape of a mound, and imitates the arc of hard palate, situated above it. When we say that the tongue "does this or that", what we really mean is that the starts the process of passing from the u (oo) or o (oh) vowels to an open i (ee) vowel, automatically and undeniably *imposes these maneuvers on the tongue, and the singer is obliged to follow their guiding influences.*

In the post *Bel Canto* period, a given *focal point* was called, in Italian, *un gancio,* or *a hook.* As the singer attempted to attach the muscles of the chest voice *(laryngeal),* to a given head voice *(pharyngeal)* hookup point, the old master-teachers would instruct him to "gather up the chest voice's power into a thinner, extremely version of itself, then direct it, using the breath stream, toward its "tiny" *gancio,* i (ee) vowel's hookup point".

Of course, the locations of the hookup points vary, relative to the pitch being sung. A *hookup point* may be located within the mouth-pharynx cavity, or further upward, above it, inside either the nasal cavities, or the head cavities of the skull.

All the tones located below middle C, downward in the singer's range also possess precise hookup points. They are much like their upper counterparts, in the upper range. However, they are much easier to locate and easier to produce. However, they do not reveal their precise spot, until after the singer has acquired all the upper hook up points, located above middle C, and all the way to the top of the singer's range, since they are dependent upon the upper range's having finally "settling down".

The "Witch's Voice", or "voce di strega"

One of the unusual transitory phases which the detached i (ee) falsetto vowel's sound goes through, as the singer applies increasing amounts of breath pressure to it, is called the *witch's voice,* so named by the early Italian voice teachers because of its strident, unmusical timbres. The *witch's voice* should be welcomed by the singer, *as it marks the* beginning of the end of the *"closed phase"* of vocal training. At the beginning of this new, "open phase" the developing falsetto i (ee) vowel leads the singer to produce many transitory sounds which are *loud, edgy, strident and shrill*, but despite these factors, they are, nevertheless, progressive and correct sounds, and the precursors of the great *squillo* tones of a first-rate singer.

The Italian term *squillo* means to *"blare",* in the manner of a trumpet. *Squillo* tones truly *"skyrocket"* over the orchestra, and outward into the theater. Only those singers who have subjugated the power of the chest voice's force and successful transported it upward in the range into the *passaggio's* tones, then past it, to the *Top Range* are privileged to possess *squillo* tones.

Gradually, the strident timbres of the *witch's voice* mellow. All the tones of the detached falsetto grow sweeter and come to possess "beautiful, *humming air currents of breath and tone"*. However, they do not convey to the singer's listeners that the *vocal cords* and the *muscles of the top register* are sustaining a great deal of breath pressure to produce these sound, *without* causing the singer difficulty in controlling them. The singer now possesses the ability to launch any note of his top range, out into the audience, in an impressive *squillo* manner.

These *squillo* tones are most compatible with the i (ee) and e (eh) vowels. But with advanced development the o (oh) and a (ah) vowels also come to possess the *"ringing and projecting"* qualities and attributes of *squillo* tones.

Advanced success with the swelled-tone exercises, is a sure sign that the *mixed voice* mechanism will soon appear. The master teachers of the past labeled the shrill, transitory sounds resulting from seemingly endless applications of the *messa di voce, the witch's cackle*. This *witch's cackle* has great affinity with the i (ee) vowel, and the raw *"witch voice"* sound of an (ah) vowel can be experienced through sounds of the words, *hat, cat, sat, bat, mat.* For amusement, tenors can easily imitate the *witch's cackle* with their upper notes, with the i (ee) vowel, by producing some shrill Hee-hee-hee! sounds, or nasal sounds like *hat, cat, sat, bat, or mat.*

It is interesting to note that when both male and female singers are singing, but they cannot be seen by their listeners, when they produce the *witch's cackle*, their voices sound so alike, that it is hard to tell which sounds are produced by the male or the female singer. This demonstrates how, in certain *"overlapping"* sections of the vocal ranges of male and female singers, they produce many similar vocal sounds.

As the *"witch's voice"* develops further, its sounds continues to mellow. Their transition from an undesirable quality to a superior one (the *mixed voice),* instructs the singer as to the nature of the various muscular techniques he may then use, for producing a variety of superior vocal sounds. For example, when a singer starts a selected, mixed voice controlled tone, with a soft, closed, velvety quality, it possess the potential of fully opening up to a loud tone, that possesses the brilliant resonant power of the chest voice. And, by modifying or *"rounding off"* the unpleasant shrillness of a *"witch voice"* tone, using a *dark* u (o) vowel it can be transformed into a superior, beautiful sound. When the singer learns to apply all the potential muscular maneuvers of the *mixed voice,* which initially made its first appearance, in the form of the *"witch voice",* it gives the singer a wide range of "vocal colors" with which to fulfill all the varying emotions of any vocal selection's dramatic intentions.

Figure   1

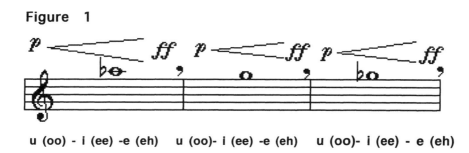

u (oo) - i (ee) -e (eh)   u (oo)- i (ee) -e (eh)   u (oo)- i (ee) - e (eh)

Three swelled-tone exercises to be used in preparation for the *esclamazio viva* exercises that follow.

Figure 2

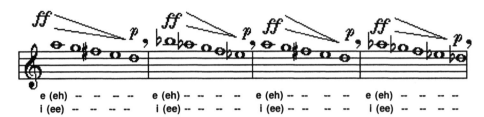

e (eh) -- -- -- --   e (eh) -- -- -- -- --   e (eh) -- -- -- -- --   e (eh) -- -- -- -- --

i (ee) -- -- -- --   i (ee) -- -- -- --   i (ee) -- -- -- --   i (ee) -- -- -- --

The "mixed voice"

As the falsetto's muscles increase in strength, through repeated applications of the swelled-tone exercise, they eventually become strong enough to thread all the chest voice's power through the falsetto starter-tone's focal point. When this is possible, the singer then possesses a new, strong, muscular mechanism for precisely controlling the actions and tonal qualities of both the registers, and with every pitch of his complete vocal range. This mechanism was called the mezzo-falso, by the early Italian voice teachers and the *voix mixte,* by the French. However, it is not available to the singer until after the antagonistic responses of each register toward the other has been mollified.

While mollifying the "raw" energy of the chest voice, with the swelled-tone exercises, the falsetto voice undergoes a radical change it its basic sound. It abandons its original "false" and "unnatural sound", shrinks in size, and becomes "sweet", "puffy", and very musical sounding. Further development causes all its former "raw sounding" tones to sound like miniature versions of the chest voice's tones. Yet, these advanced developed falsetto miniature tones have retained their original falsetto muscular controls, now greatly advanced in strength, so that the singer can easily perform the swelled-tone exercise, with all the five vowels. *NB:* Henceforth, we will refer to the *mezzo-falso* as the mixed voice.

Another noteworthy factor about the *mixed voice* is that, although it facilitates the uniting of the two registers, the two registers themselves remain forever *two different entities,* apart from the *mixed voice,* and both function separately and simultaneously, with the "separate controls" of mixed voice.

When the *detached falsetto* grows in strength to the point that it *"invites"* the actions of the *mixed voice,* there remains a subtle difference between the two. To make a distinction between *mixed voice and the detached falsetto,* the singer should closely observe the different percentages of *breath support* that is demanded of the singer, in order to produce each of them, separately. The *detached falsetto* requires a *small amount of breath support.* But, *the mixed voice requires much more, by comparison,* almost as much as when the full chest power has been added to any given tone. Only the singer *(or another singer who also possess it, or a truly qualified voice teacher),* can distinguish the difference between the *detached falsetto* and the *mixed voice,* merely by sound. This is because, in their advanced stage of development, they both sound rather alike.

Another, less ideal approach to *connecting the full chest voice power* to the advanced falsetto muscles is by the *esclamazio viva* exercise. This is temporarily available for those singers who still find it difficult to start a given tone softly, with the *mixed voice.* The *esclamazio viva* usually appeals to singers with large voices. And to those tenors who have been wrongly categorized as baritones, and who are trying to covert to being a tenor.

Figure 3

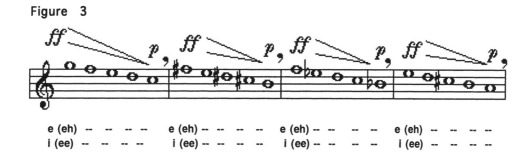

| e (eh) -- -- -- -- | e (eh) -- -- -- -- | e (eh) -- -- -- -- | e (eh) -- -- -- -- |
| i (ee) -- -- -- -- | i (ee) -- -- -- -- | i (ee) -- -- -- -- | i (ee) -- -- -- -- |

Before attempting to perform the exercises of the *esclamazio viva of Figures 2 $ 3, (above),* the singer is strongly advised to first perform some of the *preparatory* exercises, of *Figure # 1 (page 78).*

Selecting one of *Figure #1's* exercises, the singer establishes a single, sustained note, chosen from his top range, with the advanced falsetto voice, while using a breathy u (oo) vowel. Then slowly, without taking a new breath, he should change the u (oo) vowel to an i (ee), then to an e (eh) vowel. He then abruptly terminates the note, rather than diminishing it, in the usual way. After this has been accomplished, he must mentally recall the throat-position of the *ff* e (eh) vowel tone. With it's image in mind, he should understand the proper form (throat-position) necessary for performing the dynamic *ff* "attack" of all the first notes of the exercises of *Figures #2 & #3.* With the descending scales of *Figures 2 & 3,* the singer must direct the *"attack"* of the first tone's *ff* e (eh) vowel, precisely to the same throat position achieved by the exercises of *Figure #1.*

After each descending scale of *Figs. 2 & 3* has been performed with the *ff* e (eh) vowel, the singer should repeat the same scales, but this time using the fully open throated i (ee) vowel achieved by thinking of placing a "silent" open throated a (ah) vowel before the i (ee) vowel, instead of the e (eh) vowel. This i (ee) vowel scale, following so closely after the performance of the e (eh) vowel scales, will *"fine tune"* the first e (eh) vowel scale (*when repeated),* if sung correctly. However, when performing the second scales, with the i (ee) vowel, the signer must be sure that he does not focus the tone incorrectly *"forward"* into the mouth cavity, or stop the breath flow.

He must focus the i (ee) vowel *backward and upward,* behind his soft and hard palates. The i (ee) vowel will reveal to the singer the proper proportions of *head voice softness* and *chest voice power* which the e (eh) vowel tone, with its *ff* dynamic, must possess. Often, with such *"awkward" ff* attacks, the *vibrant* power of the chest voice tends to overwhelm the *head voice* controls. If that happens the singer must reduce the *ff* intensity of the exercise "attack" to a lesser, *f* dynamic.

After performing a good many successful *esclamazio viva* exercises with the e (eh) vowel, it is frequently discovered that the *o (oh) vowel* has greatly improved. The singer should set these difficult *esclamazio viva* exercises aside, then rest his voice for a day or so. When he returns to his practice sessions, he must perform simpler scales with a *p dynamic,* with a descending scale pattern, using only the *breathy u (oo) and the hollow (oh),* accompanied by a generous flow of breath.

Cracking a tone

In the not too distant operatic past, some of the finest singers of the day passed through a period of vocal development when they occasionally "cracked" a tone, on stage, before the public. This cracking assuredly embarrassed the singer, but it did not overly alarm him, nor the audience, because he and they knew well it was not injurious. And, that it was a common occurrence with other professional singers, passing through this same transitory phase of their vocal development. Very few contemporary singers are heard "cracking" a tone in public, not because they are superior vocal technicians, than those singers of the past, but because few of them are attempting to establish the proper proportions of the *head voice and chest voice power,* contributions, to each and every tone of their complete vocal range. With contemporary singers, who are do not attempt to employed the appropriate, maximum chest power in their upper range, there is less risk of them cracking a tone.

The majority of present-day student-tenors do not possess sufficient vocal structuring knowledge to correctly infuse their upper tones with ringing, projecting chest voice power, or more accurately stated, more brilliance of the vocal cords' vibrato action. Those few tenors who can manage to sing the operatic repertory, at all, are usually those lucky individuals who have discovered their head voice *(or falsetto voice),* in childhood, and have sung lyrically and well, with it, for many years.

When these lucky young students, who already have some experience with the head voice's muscular controls, seek out a competent voice teacher, and begin to study voice, seriously, they are advantaged, by their earlier years of singing with the head voice register's controls. They, are more easily likely to discover the correct way of adding the full, vocal cord's brilliant *vibrato action* all the tones of their complete range.

Present-day tenors, working on their voices alone, or in collaboration with a voice teacher, purposefully resist the full transfer of the chest power to the upper tones of there voice, knowing full well that it is a most difficult and time consuming task. If the singer progresses to a point that he feels secure and confident to essay a complete operatic role, but in a very lyrical fashion, in order to play it safe, he may get by with that approach for a little while. But he will eventually arrive at a crisis point, with his "guarded, lyric" singing, wherein the full power of the chest voice will fully assert itself. If and when that happens, the singer can only survive the crisis by learning all the required structural factors that he can, about the detached falsetto voice, and the methods of restricting the negative chest voice, in the lower range, in order for him to gradually and safely transfer limited amounts of the difficult to manage chest voice power, into all the pitches of his former, lyric tenor range.

The "inverted" tone

As the tones of the tenor's range from middle C, *upward* advance in their development, the lower tones, from middle C *downward*, become more difficult to muscularly manage, and to match, with the tones above middle C. If the falsetto controls have also been strengthened and that strength carried downward in the range, to all the tones below middle C, downward, singer may resolve all of these tone's problems and conflicts may be resolved by *inverting* all these lower tones' vowel, throat-positions away from their *chest voice orientation*, and over to new *"inverted"* throat-position placements, which are *head voice oriented.*

A properly positioned *inverted tone* is often described by the singer's listeners as being *"rounded", "effortless", "professional sounding", and "floating".* These descriptions, while being technically vague, are rather well applied. However, the singer needs more specific technical information, in order for him to accomplish the task of "inverting" of all the tones of his complete range, especially the lower range, which are often *"prisoners"* of the *negative, unblended chest voice.*

Whenever the lower range's incorrectly functioning tones, from middle C downward, render the singing voice totally dysfunctional, it becomes critical for the singer to *invert* all of them. This need is clearly communicated to the singer when he can no longer evoke any of the tones below middle C. The usual cause for these tones becoming frequently dysfunctional is because for far too long the singer has incorrectly use the muscles of ordinary speech, which are related to the raw "unmixed" the chest voice a (ah) vowel. For these lower tones to be inverted to new, correct throat "head voice" position, which will render them harmonious with the tones from middle C upward in the range, they must all be made to operate in a throat position of the u (oo) vowel, of the upper register, by utilizing the purest, detached falsetto u (oo) vowel, as exercises. These exercise will first release these lower tones from their imprisonment by the chest voice's raw, chest voice's muscular controls, *and gradually convert them all into mixed voice tones.*

　　Below are several single, sustained-tone exercises that help the tenor accomplish the inversion process with all the tones of his *lower range* from middle C, downward, to lowest note that he can sing with quality of tone, and pure vowels. With each individual lower note, the singer must perform a smooth passage from a breathy falsetto u (oo) to the more open throated o (oh) vowel, then pass on to the still more open-throated AW vowel. All of these exercises must be started with an exaggerated flow of the breath, that is released in the manner of a deep, emotional *"sigh"*. Each of these three vowels the u (oo), o (oh) and AW, will adjust the singer's throat to a new throat-position that is appropriate to the vowel being presently sung, and " invert' that particular pitch's throat-position.

　　During the course of transiting through this particular vowel sequence, while the singer is adjusting his throat socket from the u (oo) vowel, to the more open-throated o (oh) vowel, then the AW vowel, he must mainly allow the air flow to accomplish this vowel change. After all the above has been successfully accomplished, the singer should rest his voice for while. When he continues to exercise his voice again, all of these newly *inverted lower tones* must be brought into precise harmony with the pitches of middle range—*C, D♭, D♮ and E♭ and E♮.*.

　　From then on, while singing or vocalizing, the singer should discontinue "pronouncing" any of his vowels with the *muscles of ordinary speech;* the speaking voice's muscles being situated from B♮ below middle, C downward to the bottom of his range. *Instead,* he must <u>re</u>position all the throat positions of the tones—below B♭ below middle C—to new, "upside down" or "inverted" throat-positions.

　　All inverted tones are pronounced by the pharyngeal muscles *(the falsetto tones' muscles)*, in the same manner that a ventriloquist pronounces all his words, while attempting to keep his lips closed, so that his audience is distracted away from himself, and their attention focused upon his "dummy" partner, whom he wishes them to believe is doing all the talking.

　　When a tone has truly been transformed into *an inverted tone*, the singer can confirm that fact to himself by starting a selected tone very softly, with the falsetto voice, and a breath falsetto u (oo) vowel or the AW vowel, swell its volume, thereby bringing into play the power of the chest voice. Then without taking a new breath, diminish the same tone back to a soft volume, completely *releasing it from all of the chest voice power.* Successfully accomplishing this reveals that a correct inversion of any selected tones has been correctly accomplished. A non-inverted tone can only activate the chest voice's power, therefore it would not allow the singer to start it with a soft, *head-voice* dynamic, swell it, to add the chest voice's power to it, then diminish the same tone back to it softest volume.

　　Inverting *all* the tones of the complete vocal range, particularly those of the bottom, range is complex in nature. It requires an extended period of time and much practice to understand and accomplish. The singer must take special note that *it is not merely an abstract mental concept,* but rather *a tangible muscular accomplishment.* The inversion process is a radical departure from ordinary speech. Inverting all the tones of the vocal range can only be fully realized by channeling the vibrant, raw energy of the chest voice through the throat space of an advanced developed u (oo) vowel or hollow o (oh) vowel. This requires ultimate mastery in applying the breath force since there can be no tone produced and sustained, in an inverted position, if the breath supply is diminished or *"cut off"* from it. Throughout the process of inverting all tones, the breath must flow freely and continuously. If it stops, even momentarily, the tone will fall away from the process of being inverted, and be reclaimed by the muscular controls of the chest voice.

Some individuals believe that inverted tones can be created by a *"dropped jaw"* and/or *"a stretching of the throat"* maneuver. Both of these approaches are incorrect and preposterous, when compared to the correct method of creating inverted tones. Neither method, utilizing the "open throat" nor "dropped jaw" approach to inverting a tone, are generative, but solely responsive, and symptomatic. Inverted tones can only be created by correct registers' interactions, which, in turn, set up a correct " open throat" position, and "loose and freely mobile tongue and lower jaw responses."

The "Vocal Platform"

When the pitches of middle *C, C#, D♮, D♯, and E♮* reach their maximum development, they automatically group themselves very closely together, as if they were a single unit, and they form the *Vocal Platform. Above* this platform are located all the singer's *top notes. Below it* are located all the singer's *lower notes.* Each of these "platform tones" must a be capable of expanding from minimum to maximum volume, then be returned to minimum volume again, and with each of the five (5) classic vowels. The vocal platform's tones are accomplished by perfecting the swelled-tone exercise. First, by wining over the detached falsetto u (oo) vowel, strengthening it to is maximum potential, then the i (ee) vowel, then the e (eh) and the o (oh) vowel. But the "vocal platform" doesn't make itself clearly known to the singer until the fully opened-throated a (ah) vowel can be swelled to maximum volume and returned to minimum vocal, and with any or all five of these half tones of the *vocal platform,* too.

The "fully open-throated (ah) vowel" is the most difficult to accomplish, since it automatically brings into play the maximum percentage of positive, chest voice action with all of its tones. and allows the singer to diminished each individual tone back to the softest *ppp dynamic.* Achieving the open-throated a (ah) vowel with the platform's tones has a potential for granting the singer fully "open throated" tones in his upper range, from F♮ above middle C, upward to high C, and in the lower range from B♮ below middle C, downward. This open throated a (ah) vowel, should be based on the pronunciation of the words *hot, pot, lot, not.* To assure the singer that his new, open-throated a (ah) vowel are correct, he should test the accuracy of each platform tone by performing the exercises on *page 96,* with all of them.

And "open throat" vocal production means that after achieving the "open throat" positions of all the tones of the complete range, the air flow, which is so critical for superior singing, may flow fully and freely, from the bottom of the singer's range, through the *platform's tones,* and pass freely, further upward, to the top of the singer's range.

During this "open throated" stage of development, the singer comes to understand that the tones located *above* the platform, from F♮ above middle C upward, (the *middle C included),* become the *louder area of his complete vocal range.* And all the tones downward, and *below* the platform, from B♮ below middle C, become the *softer area of his complete range.*

Anthony Frisell—82

This *does not* mean that the low tones, *below the vocal platform*, should not be sung with a loud volume, when that is appropriate, nor that *high tones, above the vocal platform*, should not be sung with a *soft volume*, when that is appropriate. It means that, for the greater portion of any singing endeavor, a song, or an operatic aria, or an entire opera, *the singer must subdue the volume of his lower tones*, and with prudent judgment, and *allow for the full vowel of the tones in the upper range*. When the musical score indicates that a high tone must be sung softly, the full power of the tone *is not abandoned*, to accomplish that dynamic, but merely held back, by the muscles of the *mixed voice*, while the *soft*, falsetto component of the tone is displayed to the audience, and the loud component of the tones remains cryptically silent and momentarily restrained.

Generally speaking, we do not hear a broad range of soft and/or loud dynamics being sung by present-day singers, especially with high tones. This is because most contemporary singers have *not* had the lower octave of their vocal range restructured by the "inversion process", which subjugates the raw volume of the chest voice, to the controls of the head voice muscles. Accomplishing that allows the singer to restrain the power of the chest voice in his bottom range, and sing through the passaggio's tones with a choice of either a soft volume or a loud volume, then when singing above the passaggio, from F♮ above middle C, to the very highest note of the top range, to allow for a full-volume dynamic, free play. Most contemporary students instead, subdue the volume of the chest voice, with soft, "velvety" but "falsely sung", *pp tones*, that *are not* properly converted to upper register muscular controls, and are merely "muted" and under-structured "raw" chest tones. When ascending the range, most present-day tenors, wait until they have passed above the E♮ above middle C, to sing with any full volume. The singer may get by with this, in the beginning of his singing endeavors, but some time later, these "forged" velvety soft tone lower notes, being in reality suppressed and underdeveloped version of the "raw" and "unmixed" chest voice's controls, *involuntarily* rise upward in the range above middle C, and erode all the platform tones, and then they close down the singer's entire top range.

The solution for this problem is for the singer to bring all these soft, underdeveloped "velvety" *pp* tones below middle-C, downward to the bottom of the range, to a new state of *conversion*, and fully "open throated" tones, by many applications of the exercises on *page 96*. *But not open* to the same degree of openness as the platform tones, nor the fully open throated tones, located above the platform. But *"open throated"*, in a manner that is appropriate to their muscularly harmonious relationship to both the middle range, and the top range. Solving the mystery of correctly structuring the lower notes of the tenor's range, from middle C, downward, can be resolved, in part, by knowing which vowels to apply to them, when to apply them, and how to "pronounce" them, or and establish their correct throat-sockets. Experiment with the hollow u (oo) and o (oh) vowels, and the AW vowel, with these lower tones, and temporarily exclude the i (ee) and e (eh) vowels.

The "raw sound" of the a (ah) vowel, when pronounced, in a fully open throat manner, like the word "at"

Understand this, that all "subdued", underdeveloped notes of the singer's lower range have been deprived of their full developmental potentials by incorrect structuring, due to the lack of specific knowledge as to how to properly structure them. To *restructure* them away from the negative, underdeveloped state described above, *the singer must sometimes apply slightly radical means.* Meaning, to overcome the lower notes "dark", "thick", "covered" weak chest voice's muscular restrictions, the singer must employ the "witch voice's" pronunciation of the fully open a (ah) vowel, which is based on the raw and unmusical sounds of the fully open-throated positions, found in the words, *at, hat, pat, sat, cat.*

Or, as one famous, New York operatic coach once advised one of my students to do. Looking up at the singer from his piano, after the singer had repeatedly failed to understand the exact pronunciation of the a (ah) vowel of a certain low tone, which the coach was trying to get him to sing, the despairing coach said to him, "Pronounce the notes of your lower range in the manner of a "Boston a (ah)!"

And, the coach was right, since his suggested "Boston" a (ah), is similar to the pronunciation of the words *at, hat, pat, sat, cat,* which when slightly exaggerated, is the witch voice's version of the ideal a (ah) vowel. But the coach's good advice must be qualified, in that, the use of the "Boston a (ah)", and the *"raw"* pronunciation of the *at, hat, pat, sat, cat* words, *is only be a temporary tool*, used to extricate the lower notes out of their "dark and slumbering, chest voice cocoon," then the "Boston a (ah)," must be put aside.

After these lower notes have been *"pried away"* from the restricted controls of the chest voice's they should *be rounded*, using the hollow o (oh) vowel for a brief period of time, then rest the voice. Upon returning to the exercises, of sing the new a (ah) vowel, using the pronunciation the ideal a (ah) vowel should be passed through the throat-socket of the o (oh) vowel. Then after doing that for a while, rest the voice again, and upon returning to vocal exercises, go directly to the a (ah) vowel using the pronounce found in the words, *hot, pot, not, and God*.

A majority of English speaking vocal students, when first instructed to use the *at* pronunciation, find it difficult to believe that, by applying its "raw", "unmusical" "untraditional" vocal sounds, they will thereafter be granted beautiful, rounded, properly functioning vocal tones. Well, they will be proven wrong, but only if they temporarily summit to the use of the *at, hat, pat, sat, cat* pronunciation of the a (ah) vowel, as described above, for short periods of time.

Manual Garcia, père, is reported to have said, about such extremely bright and open vocal timbres, situated below middle C, "... the *open* and bright *timbre* demands a long, patient, and careful study from singers who have *veiled* their organ too much."

Garcia, when then asked by one of his students, if the quality of sound of the bright *open throat timbre* was not excessively shrill? He responded, "Yes, but once the organ has been formed to the excessive *clear timbre,* applying a slight veiled quality of the o (oh) and/or u (oo) vowels, will then suffice to relieve the sound of its shrill, sharp quality."

After having submitted to the *at, hat, pat, sat cat* pronunciation of the a (ah) vowel exercises, for a least a week, from B♮, below middle-C, excluding all other exercises, the singer should rest the voice for a few days. Upon returning to his exercises, should perform the following exercises, using the vowels prescribed for them *in the illustration below.*

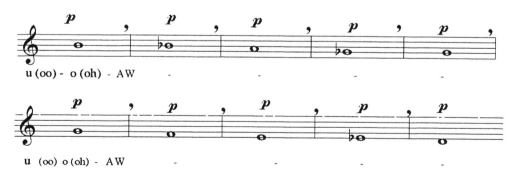

The Vocal Platform

Once the singer is in possession of the advanced developed tones of the *Vocal Platform*, the muscular movements required for *pronouncing the vowels* and *consonants* accurately become greatly reduced. While *speaking,* the muscles which accomplish basic "pronunciation" of the vowels and consonants make broad muscular movements, to accomplish their task. These broad muscular movements, where "pronunciation" of the singing vowels and consonants are concerned" are inappropriate!

However, the existence of the *Vocal Platform* allows the singer to *"gather" and "reduce"* their original, broad, clumsy movements into a *"compressed"* form. The singer is then able to concentrate his efforts almost exclusively upon the production of a selected pitch's *tone* and *vowel*, which are the greater challenge.

The illustration *below* shows the tones of the tenor's *Vocal Platform* or *passaggio.* At advanced levels of training, *these tones benefit most from the use of the hollow u (oo) vowel and o (oh) vowel.*

Another important benefit granted by possessing a well developed *vocal platform* is that, while singing any its *five halftones* middle *C♮, D♭, D♮, E♭ and E♮,* the singer is able to *prejudge* any of their individual needs of either chest voice or the *head voice'* participation, then properly regulate whichever precise amount that he has been decided upon, seconds before singing these tones. With this advantage, all vocal tones and phrases originating within the vocal platform*'s range (middle C to the E♮ above it),* and moving *further upward,* toward any higher tone (s), or *downward toward* to any lower tone (s), can be quickly *"fine tuned",* thereby avoiding any undesirable, clumsy malfunctions. The singer is not privileged to completely understand the structural nature of the vocal platform's tones, nor all their benefits, *until all of them* have reached their fullest, advanced state of development.

The Vocal Platform

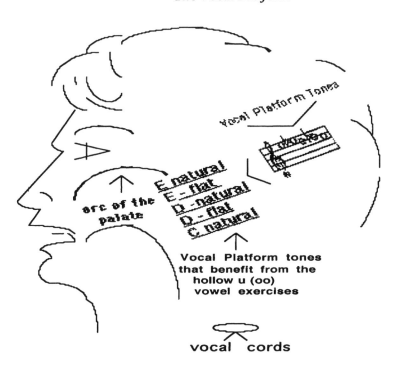

The "hollow u (oo) vowel" and how it relates to

We may best understand *the hollow u (oo) vowel* and its benefits by first comparing it to *the standard u (oo) vowel.* The standard u (oo) vowel is the only version of the u (oo) available to singers at the start of their vocal training. The standard u (oo) vowel starts off as the weakest, least revelatory, least vibrant, and seemingly most inconsequential of the five vowels. Its most important contribution to the singer is that is allows him to establish the *purest form* of the "head voice", and the ability too *"erase"* any negative muscular aspects of a selected tone which has been *"corrupted"*. The standard u (oo), when properly pronounced, possesses this ability because it allows the singer to readily access the breath flow, or motor force, necessary for producing all vocal sounds. It allows the singer to start any and all vocal tones with minimum volume and with *no participation of chest voice power.* Anatomically speaking, it has the ability to access only the first layer of the vocal cords' participation with any and all tones, while simultaneously rendering the other two layers of the vocal cords participation, necessary to produce *"full voiced" tones*, passive. With advanced development, the u (oo) becomes *the* vowel which can bring the entire vocal instrument to the highest level of *"professional polish".*

The *standard u (oo) vowel* is incapable of attaining its maximum potential strength until after both the i (ee) and e (eh) vowels have greatly advanced in strength. Only then does the standard u (oo) reveal its own individual, maximum strength, which is very different in its *"sound"* and *"behavior, "*from the strength*, "sound" and "behavior"* of the other four vowels. The advanced u (oo) vowel's strength never manifests itself with a fully open throat position, nor does it ever take on the same brilliance as the other four vowels. Seeking volume, many singers incorrectly *"widen"* the throat position of the standard u (oo) vowel toward the throat space of the o (oh), or the a (ah) vowel. *This is a misguided effort!* In reality, the u (oo) vowel's maximum "strength" and "volume" can only be obtained *when the u (oo) is kept in a very narrow beam of focus*, and relates to the *narrow focus* of the i (ee) vowel. While singing the advanced u (oo) in that manner, especially with all the tones of the *passaggio,* the singer must assure that *the tone is accompanied by a full, free flow of breath.*

The u (oo) vowel always retains a less brilliant quality than the other four vowels, and *that aspect of its individuality must always be respected.* When the u (oo) vowel is incorrectly forced to respond like an o (oh) or a (ah) vowel, an essential muscular ingredient *(and superior quality), is totally* removed from the singing voice. This deprives the singer of the ability to *"sing-talk",* technically known as *la voce canta-parlando,* meaning, a *singing-like speaking style*, so necessary for fulfilling the intimate vocal passages in songs and the recitative passages of operatic arias. *La voce canta-parlando (often refereed to as cantilena),* allows the singer to merge all the linguistic inflections of normal speech with any given tone(s), through proper use of the u (oo) vowel's *cantilena* controls, so that the words of the musical piece being sung, may possess a *linguistic authenticity* that brings the drama of that piece to life.

The "hollow" o (oh) vowel

When the standard u (oo) reaches its most advanced state of development, it grants the singer the *hollow o (oh) vowel.* The hollow o (oh) vowel differs from a traditionally sung o (oh) vowel in that, when the traditional o (oh) vowel is being sung it can operate in two mode: *Mode #1,* the *"open mode"* of the o (oh) allows the singer to keep that vowel's throat-space fully open, and facilitate him channeling a great deal of breathe flow through it. To "repair" a corrupted pitch, the singer should repeated apply the hollow u (oo), to a *"damaged" or "blocked"* tone until he feels that the tone has been restored to its full purity and health. Generally this can not be accomplish in one repair session, but by be done by several application of the hollow o (oh) vowel, then periods of resting the voice, then returning judiciously to the hollow o (oh) vowels until success in repairing a tones has been had.

In its *1st mode*, the hollow o (oh), behaves similarly to the hollow u (oo), only it is permits the singer to exert a stronger breath stream, to a corrupted tone, since it possesses a *larger vowel throat-space* than does the hollow u (oo). When in the hollow o (oh) *vowel #2 mode* of operation, it possess a high potential for *readily and smoothly* merging with the *vibrato action of the chest voice,* and allowing him to once again add *"solidity", "bite", "ring" and "brilliance",* to a corrupted pitch, thereby revealing the hollow u (oo) vowel's effectiveness in accomplishing the much desired, *"reparatory task".*

However, the hollow o (oh) greatest contribution to all singers is that is has the ability "to round" and " soften" all "raw", undesirable timbres of any and all the singers tones, away from harsh and/or shrillness which, which the "unblended" a (ah) vowel in strongly prone to exert upon any tone to which it is applied. The hollow o (oh) vowel, like the hollow u (oo) vowel, are two of the singer's *damage control tools!"*

The *hollow o (oh) vowel* accomplishes *"vocal damage control"* through applying the strongest possible breath flow to any *"damaged",* or *"dysfunction tone(s)".* Applying the hollow o (oh) "tool" is the only way the singer has of <u>undoing</u> muscular "knots", or *"improper muscular connections"* between one or more notes, or one of more Vocal Zones. When therapeutically accomplishing this task, the singer is obliged *to not* vocalize or sing. He is only allowed to apply an exaggerated flow of breath, through the use of the hollow o (oh) vowel, to any tone (s) he deems is needy of vocal repair, then rest his voice for a good while, then apply more of the same. The advanced hollow u (oo) and hollow o (oh) vowels, when they are made available through advanced muscular development, are unique "vocal repair tools" that are available to the singer throughout his entire professional career.

One must always relate the advanced developed o (oh) and the u (oo) vowels to each other, and think of the hollow o (oh) vowel as a stronger version of the hollow u (oo) vowel.

Hollow o (oh) vowel exercises

Beginning with *Phase 1, (next page),* and the E♮ pitch above middle C, the singer starts the tone with a hollow o (oh) vowel, then descending the scale with it, to the lowest note of A♮, below middle C. Then he repeats the same scale, but the *second time* he employs the open e (eh) vowel. He then repeats the scale *a third time,* but with the open i (ee) vowel, completing all three exercises of *Phase 1.*

With Phase 2, he performs a slow, smooth passage through the three vowels, starting with the hollow o (oh), passing to the *open e (eh),* then finally to the *open i (ee) vowel.* This completes Phase 2.

With Phase 3, Scale # 1, When ascending the scale with the *hollow o (oh) vowel,* the singer must tolerate its "lack of focus" and its exaggerated flow of the breath stream, otherwise it would defeat the purpose of the hollow o (oh) vowel.

With *Phase 3, Scale # 2,* Establish a hollow o (oh) vowel, with an exaggerated flow of breath, pass to an open e (eh), vowel, allowing the full, solid, vibrant action of the chest voice to connect to it. Make sure that the e (eh) vowel maintains the throat space of the hollow o (oh) vowel, then perform the ascending the scale, maintaining a free flow of breath.

Also, with *Phrase 3, Scale # 3,* establish a hollow o (oh) vowel, pass on to the open e (eh) vowel, allowing the full, solid, vibrant action of the chest voice to connect to it, then change it to and open i (ee) vowel. Gather the i (ee) vowel into as narrow throat-space as possible, then ascend the scale, while directing the air stream backwards and upwards in the throat, behind the soft and hard palates.

The singer should always keep in mind that *the free flow of the breath* confirms correct vocal usage, since it allows the singer to facilely prolong any selected tones, and verifies to him that the tone is being muscularly properly produced. The *stoppage of the breath flow* signifies incorrect muscular vocal usage, and a warning of impending vocal trouble. It is critical for the singer to become completely familiar with all the various applications of the hollow o (oh) and hollow o (oh) vowels. With all modes of applying the hollow u (oo) o (oh) vowels, the singer is obliged to arrange the proper throat position necessary to produce it.

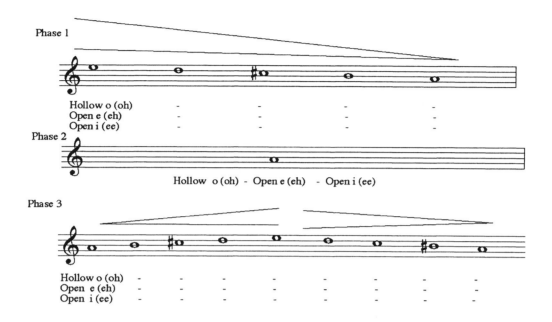

To accomplish the above, the singer should think of the ceiling of his mouth-pharynx cavity as being a large "domed roof", and that, the space below that dome must be filled to maximum capacity with wildly flowing currents of breath. The method of applying the breath flow to the lowest tones of the tenor's range, is to start any and all of them lyrically, and in the manner of a *"sigh"*. It's wise for tenors to use only the bottom E♭ and D♮, below middle C, and to descend no further in the range.

Giorgio Roncone's amazing discovery concerning the u (oo) vowel

Eventually, the *standard u (oo)* vowel develops in strength and begins to occupy the same full mouth-pharynx space as the hollow o (oh) vowels does. The singer should think of the ceiling of his mouth-pharynx cavity as being a large *"domed roof",* and that all the space below that domed roof *defines the throat space of the hollow u (oo) and hollow o (oh) vowels.* And that that full space must be filled to maximum capacity with wildly flowing breath currents. The hollow u (oo) differs from the hollow o (oh) vowel in that, it can sustain the greater impact of the breath pressure than the hollow u (oo) vowel can.

The hollow u (oo) vowel and its benefits were first discovered by the famous baritone of Rossini's time, *Giorgio Roncone (1810-1890).* It has been reported that he was the first person to unravel the idiosyncrasies of the baritone voice, as well. Before the appearance of *Giorgio Roncone* upon the operatic scene, the baritone voice, as we are familiar with it today, was unclassified as such. *Roncone* named and inaugurated this new, "baritone" vocal category. In Rossini's time, such a voice was called a *tenore forte,* or "strong-voice tenor". In fact, Rossini wrote the role of Figaro in *The Barber Of Seville* for such a *tenore forte.*

Roncone originally named these hollow u (oo) tones *vuoto,* meaning *"empty".* This term helps to describe and justify the temporary darkness and exaggerated *"empty"* throat-space of these developing tones. While the hollow u (oo) is in the process of taking muscular control, of a selected tone, away from the chest voice's muscular controls, it simultaneously reveals to the singer the tone's correct contours of the resonator space, in the mouth-pharynx cavity. It is toward this cavity's upper, posterior area, which houses each of its pitches' *focal points*, that the singer must direct and connect chest voice's power to.

Giovanni Sbriglia's "piccolo", or "tiny u (oo) vowel

After *Giorgio Roncone* discovered the *vuoto* or hollow u (oo) vowel, and explained the benefits derived from its application, another great singer-teacher, *Giovanni Sbriglia*, discovered what he called the *piccolo* u (oo) or "tiny" u (oo) vowel. *Sbriglia* achieved great results with his *"tiny" u (oo) vowel,* applying it to the *upper middle* and *top range area* of tenor voices. Doing so helped his students discover *the precise path of the breath stream must travel when leaving the lower range, entering the passaggio* at B♭ below middle C, then passing further upward to the middle C, then to the *C#, D♮, D♯, E♮,* and finally arriving at F♮ above middle C. *Giovanni Sbriglia's* "tiny" u (oo) vowels, or, in some instances, *Giovanni Sbriglia* hollow o (oh) vowel, help the singer to find the exact center of each and every tone of the passaggio, and the tiny size of there vowel throat-sockets*(the eye of the needle, so to speak),* through which the singer must pass the power of the chest voice, before connecting these tones to the chest voice's power.

Without the benefits of the hollow u (oo) vowel, the critical tones of B♭ and B♮, below middle C, plus middle C, and the C♯ next to it, would remain permanently underdeveloped, and negatively anchored to, and dominated by the chest voice. That would force the singer to produce undesirable "thick", "stiff", "monochromatic" tones, with these aforementioned pitches, as well as all the remaining pitches of the "wide passaggio", that lacked a full range of dynamics and pure vowels. Even more critical, when the aforementioned pitches remain incorrectly structured, the singer, when ascending the range and reaching the critical *lower crossover tone, B♭ below middle C, would not* be able to smoothly and correctly enter into the *passaggio. He would instead be* forced to drive the *"raw"* power of the chest voice into them. Obviously, this would cause serious damage to the *passaggio* tones.

The "gathered voice", or the "head register's' Ramp"

When all the tones of the vocal *platform* have become "gathered" closely together, the old master-teachers of the past referred to them as *la voce di gola,* or the *"voice of the throat"*. When a singer who possessed the *voice of the throat* sang any of the Vocal Platform tones (*middle C to the E♮ above it),* the selected tone communicated to him, through throat-sensations, in the upper, posterior area of his mouth-pharynx cavity, a *miniature, preview-version* of the forthcoming, fully realized tone, which the singer is about to launch outward, to his audience

The master-teachers stated that, *"unless the singer is capable of silently and inwardly hearing the correctness or incorrectness of a given tone or vocal phrase, with the aid of the voce di gola, <u>seconds before</u> he is about to deliver it to his listeners, he would never be able to sing with consistent confidence and superior tone."* Moments prior to launching a particular tone, especially a difficult one, the *voce di gola* helps the singer to precisely *pre-measure* its required breath energy, granting it not more or less than breath energy that is needed, and its precise proportional registers' needs. Voices that are incorrectly structured always demand excessive amounts of breath energy, which results in *"wasted"* energy.

Without the help of the *mixed voice* and the *voce di gola* the singer has no control over the percentages of each register's contribution to the tone (s) being sung.

The *mixed voice* allows the singer to *compress and restrict* the movements of the muscles of all the *passaggio* tones, middle C to the E♮ above it. When these tones have become *gathered*, the singer can more accurately judge the amount of *chest voice* or *head voice* needs, and "pronounce" the vowels and consonants, with such minimal, muscular movement that they appear, to the listener, to be but a single unit. Possessing the *voce racolta* is essential to signing the repertory of the *bel canto period,* and the operas of *Bellini, Rossini, Donizetti, and early Verdi.*

When a vocal phrase passes through the vocal platform, in either an ascending or descending direction, the singer is able "gathered" all its pitches into a *minimal throat-space* and with *limited* muscular movements. Doing so allows the singer to edit the percentages of chest voice power need, for any particular *passaggio* tone, otherwise the tone would respond cumbersomely. When gathered, the vocal platform tones help the singer regulate the proper strength of breath force, according to the need of the moment, and to facilely sustain a selection tone, way beyond its prescribed length of time. Otherwise the tone being sung will be immediately compromised, or stopped completely, if the breath pressure is insufficient!

When a singer whose voice has reached an advanced state of development, reflects back upon earlier phases of training and his past struggles with the breath force needs, he then realizes that during the early phase, more breath-energy was required so sing and/or exercise his voice than is presently needed. This is because advanced muscular development eliminated the division and antagonism between the two registers, and the negative bulk of the chest voice. Those were the earlier, negative factors which had caused the singer his exaggerated expenditure of the breath-force, in order to produce them.

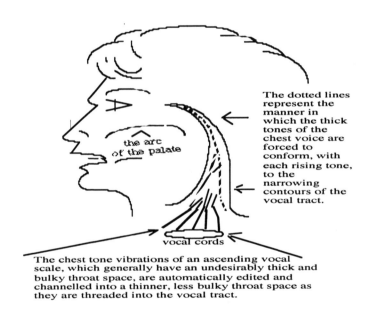

The dotted lines represent the manner in which the thick tones of the chest voice are forced to conform, with each rising tone, to the narrowing contours of the vocal tract.

the arc of the palate

vocal cords

The chest tone vibrations of an ascending vocal scale, which generally have an undesirably thick and bulky throat space, are automatically edited and channelled into a thinner, less bulky throat space as they are threaded into the vocal tract.

It has often been said that a superior singer *"listens for"* and can *"pre-hear"* the precise tone that he intends to produce, split seconds before actually singing it. True, but only for those singers who possess the *voce di gola.* The above past, historical information about *Giovanni Sbriglia, and Giorgio Rancone's* discoveries of the u (oo) vowel and the o (oh) vowel are presented, in order to awaken present-day singers to the fact that such important, detailed information is sadly lacking in present-day voice teaching methods. The u (oo) and o (oh) vowels, along with the correct i (ee) vowel, are the most misunderstood and/or inappropriately applied of all five Classic Italian vowels.

The tongue

The singer should refer back to *page 65* for information about the tongue.

The consonants

One well known dictionary describes a consonant as..."A speech sound produced by a partial or complete obstruction of the air stream by any of various constrictions of the speech organs." This description only partially explains the singer's task in pronouncing the consonants, while singing. When the singer pronounces a vowel that is accompanied by a consonant, the consonant invariably tends to interrupt the breath flow. The breath flow is vital to the correct mechanical production of the vibrations of the tone, and to accurately produce the pitch which the vowel "rides on".

To sing the best vocal tone possible, and *not allow* the consonant to interrupt the quality and accuracy of the tone, the singer must *"mute" and/or "shorten"* the pronunciation of the consonant, then pass rapidly to the vowel that accompanies it. All singers must accomplish this *"muting"* of the consonant. However, those singers whose vocal registers are underdeveloped will find this a very difficult task to accomplish. While actually singing, to shorten the time spent on producing a consonant, without compromising the vowel that accompanies it, the muscular factors that produce the tone, and the vowel must be completely independent from those muscular factors that produce the consonants.

The singer must be able to start a tone with a *pianissimo* volume *(controlled by the breath flow and the mixed voice),* so that the production of tone can be first accomplished and separately form the consonant (s) in a split second. The pronunciation of the consonant must also be accomplished rapidly and separately since, to fulfill the tone's and vowel's fullest potentials, the *pianissimo* start of the tone can only last briefly. Then the singer must quickly swell the tone to a fuller breath dynamic and phase of development, in order to quickly bring the muscular actions of the two registers into equal muscular participation.

When considering the accomplishment of these above factors: precise, pure vowel, and distinctly-pronounced consonants, *at least 99% of the effort* must be dedicated to accomplishing the precise pitch and its accompanying vowel, *and only 1%* spent on the accomplishment of the consonants.

Those singers who *have not* developed the muscular controls of both the upper and lower registers to an advanced state are forced to compromise one or more of these indispensable factors. The singer *either* manages to produce *pure vowels with an inferior tonal quality*, or a *superior tone*, with an *indistinct vowel*, or *syllables that lack distinct consonants.* With underdeveloped registers, the difficult, "closed" consonants *(b, d, f, m, n, p, s, v, y)* are often totally abandoned, or greatly muddled.

Most singers lack clearly pronounced consonants and pure vowels because the muscles of both registers have retained a great deal of chest voice weight and bulk and are still negatively related to the speaking voice, which causes the tongue to move sluggishly. Their two registers have also remained antagonistic toward each other. For the correct accomplishment of *tone, vowel, and consonants,* the negative influences of the chest voice and its antagonism toward the upper register must be completely eliminated.

The lips and facial muscles

The lips and facial muscles also participate in the production of the consonants and vowels. With the progressive development of the muscles of both vocal registers, the movements of the lips and facial muscles, like the muscles of the tongue, undergo a great many changes. They are *reassigned new ways* of functioning that are vastly different from the ways they had functioned, when they were controlled by the speaking voice's muscles. As the singer succeeds further with the *swelled-tone exercise* using the fully open a (ah) vowel, the lips and facial muscles are forced to completely abandon their relationship to the chest voice's muscle and the speaking voice, and utilize *new ways* of performing their old tasks, those that are appropriate for superior singing. During their period of change, certain exercise and the manner in which they employ any of the five classic Italian vowels, simultaneously impose upon the singer new, often exaggerated lips, tongue and cheeks movements.

For example, when the singer is strengthening the u (oo) vowel, particularly with the *passaggio* tones, the lips tend to purse and protrude forward. Sometimes, when strengthening the u (oo) vowel the singer lips may quiver or tremble, as the facial muscles, surrounding the lips, are stretched more than usual, to accommodate the new singing pronunciation of the *new* u (oo) vowel. To the inexperienced singer, these stretching, trembling and quivering responses seems extreme. With advanced development and the growing dominance of the upper register's control over all the tones of the singers complete range, especially the lowest notes, these facial and lips muscles' movements become greatly reduced, and they eventually *"settled down"* into a new state of *"normalcy"*.

It has often been said, by many accomplished singers, that during the most advanced phase of their vocal development, the movements of their *tongue, face and lips,* became greatly troublesome, and that, in order to achieve the best possible pronunciations of them, they would have to use the same method of pronunciation which superior ventriloquist use. That is to say, when the ventriloquist speaks for his *"dummy partner",* he attempts to maintain a closed-mouth position of his lips, with little movement of his cheeks and lips as possible, to conceal from his audience that, it is *not he*, but instead, his dummy-partner who is speaking.

It has been reported that *Enrico Caruso*, the great Neapolitan tenor of the past, said this: *"A few words on practicing with closed-mouth, may be appropriate. This method of study is really all that is necessary to place certain voice, but it is bad for others. When one can do it safely, however, it is a most excellent resource."*

Both the correct u (oo) vowel and the o (oh) vowel help the singer to accomplish this "closed mouth" position, of certain tones in his range. They are especially helpful for tenors who have difficulty in properly structuring their passaggio tones, since they tend "spread their lips radically" with these tones, where as the u (oo) and o (oh) vowel, tend to make them round and purse their lips forward, *"fish-mouth"* style, thereby transferring the main muscular actions for correctly producing the passaggio's tones, *to the upper, posterior area of their throats*, where they occur.

Below are some exercises for converting the lips and cheeks' movements *away from* the muscular control of the chest voice, and over to the muscular controls of the head voice. Select a B♮ pitch from the first measure of the illustration above. Slowly change the open o (oh) vowel to an open i (ee) vowel, modeling its throat shape on the open o (oh), and/or an open a (ah). During the process of changing the hollow o (oh) vowel to an open i (ee) vowel, the singer will feel his tongue automatically moving from a lower position, down low in the throat channel, to a higher one. The main body of the tongue will move into the mouth, where it crunches itself into a mound-shape that imitates the dome shape of the hard palate, just above it. Endeavoring to speak, in a regular manner, with the tongue in that position would be awkward. However, that is the precise position that the tongue must assume to accurately accomplish a correct, open i (ee) vowel, while singing.

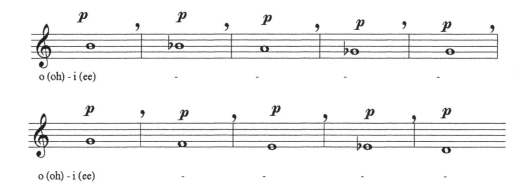

o (oh) - i (ee)

o (oh) - i (ee)

All the remaining vowels must be produced by passing them from the this transformed open i (ee) to the open e (eh), o (oh) and a (ah) vowels. While this is being accomplished with the lower tones of B♮ below middle C, downward, the singer's ordinary lips and cheeks' muscular patterns are being "denied him". And when speaking, after exercising his voice the singer finds that projecting his speaking voice is rather cumbersome. During this metamorphoses, the singer must speak softly, on all occasions. He must *not* try to reinstate his old speaking voice. It will be helpful for him to speaks in the manner of "a breathy sigh", until the complete process of transferring all the lips and cheeks movements away from the chest voice's speaking controls, over to the muscular controls of the upper register's singing muscular controls. After that has been completely accomplished, his speaking voice will have been radically and *permanently changed*. From then on, he will note that, when speaking, the breath stream, necessary for all vocal sounds, now goes immediately upward and backward in his throat, and into the resonating chamber of the mouth-pharynx cavity where it "buzzes" with every sentence he utters.

After exercise the voice with the above exercises, the singer should rest his voice for quite some time.

CHAPTER SIX

"Low larynx" position versus "high larynx" position

There exists a long-standing debate as to whether the singer should maintain a "low larynx" position or a "high larynx" position while singing. The answer is that the larynx *(like the tongue),* should *never* be made to remain in any one fixed position. It must be allowed full flexibility of movement.

There are *two major modes* of using the singing instrument, and the larynx behaves differently in each. The first is *the detached mode, wherein the larynx and the pharynx <u>are not</u> connected to each other*, usually when the voice is being exercised, and the second is *the connect mode*, when <u>*the larynx and the pharynx are connected,*</u> the *singing mode.*

When the voice is in *the detached mode,* or exercise mode, the position of the larynx should be given full, free range of movement. Sometimes it is necessary to detach the larynx from the pharynx for a particular exercise, at other times, it serves a specific purpose to connect it to the pharynx. That way, the larynx may respond appropriately to the progressive structuring process. Whichever, in both cases, each of the five instrumental vowels exerts its own particular influence upon the larynx's position.

When in *exercise mode,* using the detached falsetto, the hollow u (oo) vowel is best for correctly positioning the larynx, especially for the lower range tones, since it *does not* employ the full power of the chest voice. Upon connecting any of the remaining four vowels—the open i (ee), e (eh), o (oh), and a (ah)—to the hollow u (oo) vowel, the singer is undeniably obliged to switch to the *connected mode* of singing and "clamp" the power of the chest voice *(involving movement of the larynx),* to the tone being sung. This connected mode of singing alters the position of the larynx graphically, especially from B♮ below middle C, downward. If this *connection between the larynx and the pharynx* is not accurately perceived, physically felt, and freely allowed, it means that the singer is not employing the use of the *falsetto register* in *collaboration with his chest voice.* Therefore his larynx will *not respond correctly.* He should then read through this manual from its beginning, and try to understand the principle that states and explains why all the tones of his vocal range must be produced with the muscular controls of *both the chest and falsetto registers.*

Each individual vowel, respectively, will undeniably effect the positioning of the larynx. Setting the u (oo) vowel aside for the moment, and giving our attention to the remaining four vowels, first, the *open i (ee) vowel* is the one that will allow *only the precise amount of chest voice participation to be added to any selected tone,* and it will correctly position the larynx in accordance to the pitch being presently sung. Therefore, the remaining vowels e (eh), o (oh), and a (ah), where their correct larynx-positions are concerned, will be *tuned and directed* to its proper position by the *open* i (ee) vowel *(which differs greatly from the speaking voice i (ee)),* but only when the open i (ee)'s throat-position is based upon the hollow o (oh)) vowel, and a completely detached, falsetto oriented tone.

When exercising the open i (ee) vowel with the falsetto voice, there are many times when the detached falsetto i (ee) vowel pulls the larynx to *abnormally high positions.* These abnormally high positions are *only temporary* and must be allowed. They permit the tone being exercised to develop its correct primary structure of purity, and to find its *precise focal point,* somewhere along the length of the resonance channel, to the power factor *(contributed by the larynx).* In this way, when the singer employs the remaining vowels e (eh), o (oh), a (ah), the larynx's position, with each individual pitch and vowel, will automatically adjust to the proper height and/or depth, and find its correct *focal point* along the length of the vocal tract, which the open i (ee) vowel has prepared for it.

When the singer performs a series of ascending scales, in *the connected mode (when both registers' muscular actions are operative),* using the u (oo), the open, hollow (oh), or the rounded AW *(u, o, a vowels combined within it),* and only afterwards, an a (ah) vowel, which has been passed through an hollow o (oh) vowel, the larynx alters its position away from the extremely high position, *created by the detached falsetto open i (ee) vowel,* toward a lower position, appropriate to each of these vowels' influence upon the presently sung pitch. The singer should carefully observe the various responses of the larynx which each of the five vowels exerts upon it. When performing the forthcoming scales, the larynx's position must remain flexible so it can readily adjust to the next, higher pitch and its accompanying vowel, which is about to be sung.

The most critical movement which the larynx makes is one that *the singer must consciously instigate.* That of "readying the voice for singing", after a long period of not having sung. Generally, during brief periods of *not singing,* the larynx gradually settles away from its various connections to the pharynx, with the various pitches of the singer's range, and settles down at the bottom of the range, where it finds a position of comfort, ready and waiting for the singer to again warm up his voice. The *warm up,* obliges the singer to readjust his larynx away from its low, resting place, and reposition it at various pitches of the range, determined by the height or depth of the tone being presently exercised.

Reawakening the singing voice, and the larynx from its resting place, at the bottom of the singer's range, is best accomplished rather slowly, by starting at the top of the *middle range,* employing the breathy, falsetto u (oo) voice, and/or the hollow o (oh) voice, with a free flow of breath, using descending scale exercises, starting at E♮ above middle C. The object is to get the air flowing in the middle range *first,* then gradually add the chest power of the chest voice to these middle tones, then move warming up the top tones, then finally the bottom tones. But this precise order *should not* always be rigidly adhered to. There are times when either the bottom range, the middle range, or top range areas suggest to the singer that *it* should be *warmed up* first.

Palatal Resonance

At one time in the past, the resonance factor of the *"upper middle range"* tones, *E♭, E♮, F♮ and F♯ above middle C,* when structured in a superior manner, were referred to as possessing, when actually singing, *"palatal resonance".* This was because the singer felt the vibrations of these vocal platform tones, as the breath-force evoked them, by "gently pulsating" in the region of the soft palate, when it is positioned similarly, as when gargling with mouthwash, to cleanse the mouth. This can only occur when the singer has correctly reposition these specific *"crossover to the upper register's tones"* of the middle range, away from the chest's voice's muscular controls, and over to the upper register's muscular controls.

During the early period of voice structuring, after the falsetto register's controls have been repeatedly brought downward from the Top Range and made to "saturate the *E♭, E♮, F♮ and F♯ above middle C,* when *the singer could only produce them* with the detached and often *"muted",* falsetto voice, which produced *"opaque", "covered"* sound qualities. Their incomplete development would *not allow* the singer to add the core brilliance of the chest voice to them—especially with a fully open a (ah) vowel. When the structuring of these particular pitches advanced, the missing core brilliance of the chest voice finally became available to the singer, and these tones earlier, "closed, opaque, covered" sounds then changed to *"brilliant", "open throated"* sound qualities. In the past, the old master-teachers described this above accomplishment as *"...piercing the soft palate"* with the *"brilliance" of the chest voice, usually with the open i (ee) vowel.*

The initial task of repositioning the larynx, with the help of the swelled-tone exercise, takes a long time *(in some cases, many years)*. This is because the larynx is often found to be mired, *for a very long time,* in a rigid, inflexible position somewhere in the lower range area *(but below the first tone of the vocal platform, which is middle C)*. This undesirable situation, of possessing a *"mired larynx",* is often as a result of the singer having performed many incorrectly applied ascending scales which has forced the "raw" chest voice upward into the platform tones. However, after the long and arduous task of correctly positioning the larynx has been accomplished, warming up the voice can be accomplished within half an hour.

During the warm-up session, while repositioning the larynx, the singer *must not allow* the larynx to first position itself on any of the tones *below* the vocal platform, *below middle C.* Otherwise, *the "opening" and/or "entrance"* into the wide, upward, posterior curving sound waves passageway, leading into, and through the registers' break are, then further upward to the tones of the *Top Range* would remain closed and inaccessible. Instead of that, the singer must carefully guide his larynx toward the *first tone* of the vocal platform, middle C, *and some times even lower, perhaps the B♭ below middle C, and at other times above middle C.* He must then firmly clamp the B♭ pitch *(or whichever pitch, other than the B♭, that he has instead selected),* to the hollow throat-socket of a breathy u (oo) vowel, or to the hollow o (oh) vowel, then thread the i (ee) vowel through the *hollow* u (oo) or the o (oh), *then slowly and gently* swell the tone, in order to add the chest voice power to it. When that has been accomplished, the appropriate power of the chest voice will have been added to the tone (s), and the larynx will have bypassed the lower range area of the voice *(B♮ below middle C, downward in the range) and connect itself to any other tone, above middle C,* and then the singer may safely begin to exercise the *passaggio's* tones, then afterward, the upper areas of his range, and finally his lower tones.

Francesco Lamperti [1], one of the most eminent teachers of the post-*Bel Canto* period, identified *middle C* to be "... the *most* difficult tone in the entire vocal range with which to perfect the *swelled-tone* exercise, and with all five vowels".

William Shakespeare a famous concert and oratorio singer, teacher of singing, and one of *Francesco Lamperti's most eminent students,* wrote a well-known treatise on singing in 1921 entitled *The Art of Singing.*[2] In it, he states, "... in order to produce any note in fullness and purity of tone, *it is necessary to place or balance the larynx over the breath* and retain its appropriate position there. This involves the upward, backward pulling muscles upon the tongue-bone *(hyoid bone),* balanced by those muscles *pulling the vocal instrument downwards towards the chest bone.* "

Here are some important facts to know, relative to *low and high larynx positions*: the "upward pulling muscles upon the tongue-bone" is accomplished by the use of the open i (ee) detached falsetto

---

1—*Francesco Lamperti* (1813-1891), one of the hallowed names in the teaching of *bel canto* principles. One of his most important precepts was that "... a correctly trained voice can crescendo and diminuendo, and a voice that can crescendo and diminuendo is well placed." Some of his famous students were *Marietta Alboni, Teresa Stoltz, Maria Waldmann, Italo Campanini, and William Shakespeare.*

2— *The Art of Singing,* William Shakespeare, Ditson, New York, 1921.

vowel, after it has been threaded through a hollow o (oh) vowel, and developed, with the principles of the swelled-tone exercise. Conversely, the *"downward pulling muscles"* are controlled by the chest voice open a (ah) vowel, but more safely and musically with the open o (oh).

Frequently, contemporary teachers erroneously instruct their students to place and maintain their larynx in a *"low position"*, at the bottom area of their vocal range. This results in the student only being able to sing stiff, thick, one-dimensional tones. This mistaken concept is often applied to achieve quick results and to obtain resonant tones, or what is *falsely believe* to be "powerfully, projecting, professional quality tones."

Most singers who use the "low larynx" position method learn quickly that it is short-lived, because it excludes the all the other important participation of the upper register's muscular actions, in all tone production. The abnormally dark, thick sounds produced by a rigid, *"low larynx positioning"* is the cause of many singers being vocally and incorrectly classified, and placed into lower vocal categories, than is appropriate. One symptom of the *"lower larynx position's"* incorrectness is revealed when singers employing it *cannot* sing a pure u (oo) vowel. Their impure u (oo) vowel invariably distorts toward the sound of *"uh" or "oh"* and their i (ee) vowel remains forever thick and distorted toward an e (eh) or an a (ah) vowel.

After the singer's voice has reached an advanced state of development, there comes into existence *three separate and distinct muscular mechanisms for controlling the tones of the complete vocal range.* These three separate muscular mechanisms *(or layers of the vocal cords participation, as they are physiologically called),* are located in very close, parallel proximity to each other. These mechanisms do not exist at the beginning of the singer's vocal training, but gradually come into existence. with the gradual and proper creation of the entire *resonance channel.* Each of these three mechanisms has its own distinct, individual muscular actions and tonal qualities, and each relates to any given tone in proportion to the depth or percentage of the vocal cords' participation with the tone:

1) The *detached falsetto (detached from the power of the chest voice),* serves as the *"starter"* of all tone;

2) The *mezzo-falso*, commonly known as the *mixed voice*, which when subjected to an increase of breath pressure, brings into play an increased depth of the vocal cords' participation. This *mixed voice* mechanism controls the *addition or subtraction of the chest voice's power,* to any selected tone, which can be accomplished by the swelling or diminishing of the volume of the "starter", detached falsetto tone;

3) The *"joined together"* state of the two registers is called the *"full voice"*, a translation of the Italian term *la voce piena.* When the *full voice* is operative, there exists a maximum connection of the chest voice's muscular controls to the muscular controls of the advanced developed falsetto, with every tone of the vocal range. The *joined together state* of the two registers automatically gives any tone its *"real"* sound *(as opposed to the "false" sound, which all phases of detached falsetto usage give to any tone),* or the readily recognizable *"performing quality"* of the singing voice. When we say that the *full voice* requires a maximum connection of the falsetto voice to the chest voice's power, *we do not imply that the singer must produce the maximum volume which a tone is capable of rendering.* We merely mean that, *all* the potential uses of the singing voice *are not available to the singer until the muscular controls of both the chest voice and head voice have been put into maximum connection to each other.*

***The three separate muscular mechanisms of the advanced developed
vocal registers that control the advanced singing voice.***

1. The *detached falsetto* — *2.* The *mixed voice* — *3.* The *full voice* or "performing voice."

Figure 1

An abstract representation of the three
vocal mechanisms of control when they
are separated into layers.

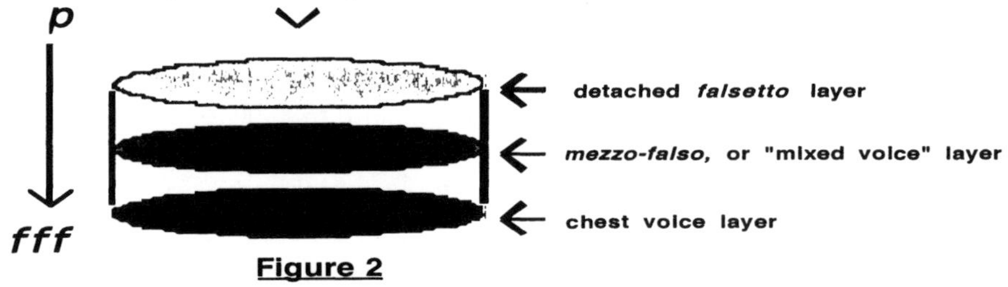

p

← detached *falsetto* layer

← *mezzo-falso,* or "mixed voice" layer

← chest voice layer

fff

Figure 2

An abstract representation of the three
vocal mechanisms of control when they are
"gathered" and brought closely together.

—— detached *falsetto* layer

—— *mezzo-falso,* or "mixed-voice" layer

—— chest voice layer

When these three mechanisms are used in unison they give the
singer the full voice or "performing voice"

It should be remembered that, they should be evoked in the precise order given below:
a) All initial vocal exercises must be aimed at developing the *detached falsetto*, which
in time, reaches an advanced stage of muscular development, and brings
  into existence—
b) The *mixed voice,* which, when achieved, automatically grants the singer control over—
c) The addition or subtraction of the chest voice power *(or "full voice")*, to all the tones
of his range, *which is the only state of the two vocal registers that will allow the singer
to perform.*

No other progressive training order of development will achieve for the singer these three
muscular controls of the singing instrument. Those singers whose training methods *do not* follow this
precise developmental order can *only* attain partial or incomplete aspects of these muscular controls. This
is because many of the tones of the singing range will *not* have been developed from *the starting point* of
the detached falsetto.

Most contemporary singers readily *seek alternative methods* of bringing the muscular actions of
the two vocal registers into play, but they are almost always compromised methods of voice building, that
fall short of *the ideal.* The most *significant missing factor* with those *"quick methods"* is that, they fail to
grant the singer the ability to *select a softly produced tone and then to pass on to a fortissimo dynamic
with it, then return to tone to its original soft dynamic.* When these critically important maneuvers *of soft
to loud and then back to soft again* are missing, there is no controlling the voice. The general, overall
quality of these voices remains forever *"muffled",* and lacking in vibrant brilliance. And, there is little
variety of tonal color with them. And, there is seldom a tone produced *(especially in the high range),*

which starts with a *fil di voce, "a thread of voice"*, which can be swelled to full volume; a vocal maneuver that is thrilling to the listener.

Because most present-day tenors *are not* properly trained with the falsetto voice, we presently have a surplus of *"thick"*, *"lack luster"* tenor voices that produce tones of inferior, monochromatic quality. Through historic recordings, the advanced *mixed voice* tones of *Beniamino Gigli, Giuseppe Di Stefano, Jan Kiepura, Nicolai Gedda, Tito Schipa, John McCormack, and Miguel Fleta,* superior tones which are frequently mistaken to be "detached falsetto tones", can be studied by contemporary tenors. With repeating hearings, present-day tenor may come to understand what is denied them, when they neglect the development of the advanced falsetto voice.

The "puffy" throat sensation of the advanced falsetto tones

After the falsetto muscles have passed through all the aforementioned developmental phases and the singer can perform a correct swelled-tone exercise, the detached falsetto voice generally undergoes many radical changes, both in sound and muscular action. Firstly, each detached falsetto tone becomes so greatly reduced in volume that the singer can only achieve its required detachment by singing with minimal volume, and assuring that it is started with an ample breath flow, resulting in a tone that is almost *a whisper*. This extreme softness of volume does not mean that these soft tones are not still correct, very strong, and capable of granting the singer a tone of *fff* dynamic.

These new, soft detached falsetto tones *(whose sounds contain elements of the singer's full volume sounds),* are accompanied by "puffy" throat sensations. *These puffy sensations are caused by swirling currents of air* which are positive indications that the muscles of both registers are finally, and totally willing to cooperate with each other, to grant the singer the beneficial aspects of both registers, and a free flowing stream of breath force. These advanced developed falsetto tones, in their extremely soft, *though not lacking in power state,* readily mergers with the power factor of the singing voice. But this positive and highly desirable potential, of these extremely soft and puff falsetto tones, is seldom detectable by the average listener, nor the average vocal student, nor, especially by the majority of voice teachers, and they are generally only clearly and completely understood by other superior singers, who also possess "expert ears".

When these puffy tones appear, the singer, at last, finds that his performance of the swelled-tone exercise has become "outstanding and impressive" and "second natured". When this is the case, the three separate mechanisms of control become so closely related or *"gathered together"* that all the tones of the vocal range begin to have an *"impacted"* quality. This means that each tone of the singer's complete range possesses a full spectrum of superior qualities and muscular controls—softness, loudness, sweetness, power, darkness, brightness, and a core brilliance that helps them to project outward, into the audience. For the singer, however, this advanced state of the *voce racolta* or *"gathered voice"* may present difficulties in preserving the *separate function and ready availability of detached falsetto controls.* Any selected *"connected tone"* (when both registers operating together), must be capable of being *freed and separated* from the participation of the chest voice's mass and weight, and to become *again,* a detached falsetto tone. This is necessary to make available the singer his required soft, starter-tone, with which to "warm up" his singing voice, after it has been resting for a day or more.

A detached falsetto tone, no matter how muscularly advanced it has grown, is the *only* sure "exercise tool" *that allows the singer, during his warm-up session, to safely call into play the power of the chest voice, and in gradual percentages.* The reason that it often becomes confusing and difficulty for the singer to evoke the detached falsetto, after all tones of the range have reached the advanced state of the "gathered voice", is because, when all three mechanisms of control reach an advanced level of muscular harmony with each other, they "prefer" to remain in that close physical proximity to each other, rather than be separated into individual "layers". *But they must be made to separate from each other*, so that the *detached falsetto mode* is always available to the singer, for each day's proper warm-up, and afterwards, for his singing. This is especially critical when the singer has to sing demanding, *"full voice"* rehearsals, of an soon upcoming performance, day after day, without proper rest periods, for his voice. The breathy u (oo) and hollow o (oh) vowel, while temporarily excluding the use of the i (ee), e (eh), and open a (ah) vowels, are particular helpful to the singer for establishing the "detached" mode of the falsetto voice. The singer who finds himself in the above situation must use the exercises found on *page 96.*

If the singer be insistent, that any selected starter-tone maintains the softest volume until he feels the "puffy throat sensations" which are associated with complete freedom from the mass and weight of the chest voice, and the free flow of the breath, then a *proper, daily* "fresh start", to the warm up process, can be had. Sometimes, only a few tones of the range will respond to the singer's insistence on establishing a correct starter, detached falsetto tone, with its free flow of breath. These few free tones are generally found with the tones of the registers' break area. When this is the case, the singer should not be alarmed by the fact that remaining tones of his range are not responding to his attempt to call the detached falsetto mechanism into play. The singer should then pass on to the full voice, or *fully connected mode* of the two vocal registers, and sing some lyric pieces.

The advanced detached falsetto tones, with their accompanying "puffy" throat sensations, usually first appear for tenors, with one or more tones above F♮ above middle C. With regards to the sensation of the breath flow, felt by the singer, usually feels the actions of the breath flow most acutely with his middle range tones, which are located within the mouth-pharynx cavity. While his breath flow sensations and perceptions of the puffy tones of his Top Range, are felt and perceived as extremely "tiny *throat-spaces into which the energized breath flows rapidly through, while producing a tiny "whistle sound".* However, none of these "tiny throat space nor their unusual tiny throat spaces and sounds ever fail to communicate to the singer their actual powerful strength, and willingness to sustain the maximum power and projection factors of the chest voice. The *"puffiness"* factor, which is physically sensed by the singer, is the result of many tiny, shimmering vibrations *(minimal vocal cord participations, or what many call the vibrations of the "thin edges" of the vocal cords),* pulsing in one or more of the resonator cavities, depending upon the pitch being sung at the moment.

These shimmering, puffy tones vibrate in maximum harmony with the complimentary vibrations of the vocal cords' *first level* of participation in creating a beautify, *"shimmering"* detached falsetto pitch. When these *"shimmering vibrations"* arrive at their appropriate resonance cavity, they completely "flood" and fill it. And then, through pleasant and harmonious throat sensations, they allow the singer to "feel-see" *(envisioning, through physical sensation),* the entire resonator cavity's precise throat-space, and the corresponding shape of the vowel being presently sung. This is done with such *mental* preciseness that no doubt remains in the singer's mind, as to the tone's accuracy and superiority. Technically speaking, these "shimmering, puffy, falsetto vibrations", in the upper resonator cavities, are in perfect harmony with a corresponding, exact adjustments of the vocal cords, far below. This harmony between the vocal cords adjustments and the upper resonance cavities sensations, communicates to the singer the precise path of vocal ascent that all chest power vibrations must take, along the length of the resonance channel, in order to arrive at their terminal "hook up" point (s) within any of the resonance cavities. It is these "puffy" sensations that give the singer a clear understanding of how the positive *(though often "raw")* power of the chest voice can be safely incorporated into a superior tone production, and produce smooth and beautiful tones that are powerful and highly controllable. This power-control-factor of the chest voice is granted to the singer by the concealed strength of the soft, *puffy mixed-voice*, which subjugates and focuses chest voice's *"unruly power"*, then "smoothes" it, and gives it a *"coating"* of beautiful sound.

The great Italian tenor and master teacher, *Antonio Sbriglia (1832-1916),* the teacher of *Jean de Reszke,* frequently utilized these tiny *"puffy"* advanced falsetto tones, with his teaching practices.

Sbriglia called them his *"tiny u (oo) tones"* and used them to identify and develop the purest form of the *passaggio* and *head tones* of his pupils. Sbriglia also used his *"falsettini"* tones *(super small)*, to develop the upper range of his students. He informed his student that "properly producing these "tiny" u (oo) vowel tones, would reveal to the singer the price path of the breath stream, with the all the *"wide passaggio's* tones, from its initial entrance at B♭ below middle C, to its top at F♮ above middle C.

The *"puffy throat sensations"* of the detached falsetto tones and *Antonio Sbriglia's "tiny u (oo) vowel"* and his "small *falsettini"* tones *are all* manifestations of the developing advanced falsetto voice. When they appear, all vowels produced by the student-singer respond in the same manner as does *Sbriglia's* single "tiny u (oo) vowel"—they are easily evoked, round, powerful, projecting, and highly controllable and above all *beautiful sounding.* Unlike *Sbriglia,* who may have only applied these puffy tones to a limited area of the singer's range, *we, on the other hand,* apply them to any and all tones of the range, according to the structural needs of the moment.

It should be noted that our advanced falsetto tones, with their accompanying *"puffy throat sensations",* are more readily available *after* the singer has sung for an hour or more, with the "connected mode of voice" of both registers, then stops singing and attempts to enter the "disconnected mode", seeking out a detached falsetto tone. In that case, when the singer has sung for an hour or so, stops singing and succeeds in detaching the power of the chest voice power from any *connected tone,* there will remain, *with the detached falsetto tone,* a lingering solidity of the chest voice which is correct, and a clear indication of how the detached falsetto itself, gradually changes and becomes increasingly more "solid". Keeping these thoughts in mind, the progressive growth of the falsetto voice, can thus be clearly and precisely monitored.

Chapter Seven

The critically important ascending scales that prepare the singing voice for performance

After the singer has satisfied most of the structural needs of the singing voice, he must put the voice to the test of actually singing. To make the voice ready for performance, selected warm-up exercises, which the singer has used up to this point, must be performed *sparingly*, then put aside, and the singer must prepare himself to actually sing.

One of the major differences between exercising the singing voice, and actually singing with it, is that while exercising the voice, the singer can select certain *preferred vowels* and certain vocal areas of the range to exercise, which he believes will accomplish a certain positive result. When actually singing, however, such choices are no longer available. While actually singing, the order of notes and the combinations of vowels become *"scrambled"*, and most often, to the singer's disadvantage. Therefore, for the singer to sing the selected musical piece at hand successfully, and simultaneously preserve the correct functions of his singing voice, he must be technically capable of successfully meeting all the vocal challenges, which the present musical piece presents to his voice, and his vocal technique.

For example, while actually singing, the entire vocal range must respond in a harmonious and spontaneous manner. It must allow the singer to produce all the assigned tones with an even, superior quality, with the five classic, Italian vowels clearly realized. The singer must also possess absolute control of the breath force's dynamics, especially with the tones of the *passaggio.*

N.B. While the singing instrument is in *performance mode,* and the singer is obliged to stop singing for a moment in order to speak, he must speak very softly. Otherwise, there is a possibility of inviting an *undesirable amount of the chest voice's power*, to the tones of the lower range. Even when not actually singing, during his day's daily routine, the singer must endeavor to speak softly, and *not* attempt to project his speaking voice, for any great distance.

Ascending vocal movement

All ascending vocal movement possesses a *potential* for permanently injuring to the singing instrument, and especially so, if the structuring of the head voice tract has not been completely accomplished. Ultimately and ideally, the advanced head voice is to be connected to the transportable power of the chest voice, to make all tones of the range function safely, and as one single unit.

Therefore, when performing the forthcoming exercises, with their ascending vocal movements, it is critical that the singer observe several factors:

1) "The upward pulls", created by the muscular development of the "detached falsetto", must be operative on each and every successive *(ascending)* tone.

2) The inherent "bulk" or "mass" of the chest voice's influence must be continuously reduced as the scale rises. This desirable reduction process, regardless of pre-structuring, can only take place if the singer makes a conscious effort to "thread" each successive tone of the ascending scale *into the thinner muscular contours of the head voice trac*t.

3) As the ascending scale approaches the *passaggio* area, Bf below middle C and up to the Fn above middle C, the singer must transfer the *"work load"* of each successive ascending tone away from the chest voice's muscular controls, and over to the muscular controls of the head voice.

The narrow, highly energized sound "beams" of the upper range

When a singer, who possesses a correctly trained voice, sings a vocal phrase that ascends to the top of his vocal range, there is an appropriately, graduated increase of projecting volume accompanying it. However, the singer perceives this increase in volume very differently than his listeners do. Unlike the wide increasing spray of voluminous tone that his listeners hear, as he ascends to the top of his range, the singer is *not* privileged to hear his voice with the same external reality as his listeners do.

The singer is instead obliged to *"feel-hear"* these tones, through his throat sensations, as to how they possible sound to others. As a phrase mounts to the top of the range, the tone in question "feels-hears" to the singer as though it were growing smaller in volume and "width". And, as though the tones of a phrase were less powerful at the top of the range, than in his middle and lower range. This discrepancy of perception, between what the singer feels and hears, and what his listeners hear and perceive, has a very logical explanation. As the singer attempts to bring the *"core solidity" and "ring"* of the chest voice to the top of his range, the singer is obliged to reduce and narrow its inherent thickness and bulk, to conform to the narrow physical shape of the upper, advanced falsetto area of his Top Range. Otherwise, precise intonation, pure vowels, beauty of tone, and control of dynamics will be denied to him.

However, the average singer is not able to directly control this necessary *"narrowing"* of the chest voice's volume and bulk. Those negative factors can only be dealt with by the muscles of the *gathered voice.* When most contemporary singers sing a phrase that mounts to the top of their ranges, the top tones of the phrase tend to narrow as did the voices of the great singers of the past. However, present-day singer tones *do not* increase in ringing, projecting power at the top of their range. Without the perfection of the swelled-tone, falsetto exercises, these singers *can not* add the maximum chest voice "core" and "ring" to their top most tones. Instead, they produce top tones that are generally small in size, limited in volume, and consistently lacking the ringing, core brilliance and focus of the chest voice. Therefore, their top tones are usually overpowered by the orchestra.

The most critical factors missing from contemporary singing are: *1) in the upper range,* the full, correct addition of the chest voice's power; and *2) in the lower range,* the use of *la voce canta-parlando (cantilena),* granted to the singer by the controls of the advanced falsetto operating fully there, which creates a large variety of tonal colors and grants the singer the ability to swell and/or diminish all of his lower range tones, and to clearly pronounce the words being sung with them with authority and authenticity, all of which give the drama vitality.

Ascending scales

We now present the extensive ascending scales which serve to collect, then gather closely together all the tones of the singer's vocal range, in preparation for singing. The singer must tailor these exercises to his individual needs. He must *not* be satisfied with readily available lower notes, when the higher notes of the range are not easy to produce. *As the voices of all singers mature, the area of the range where they feel most comfortable, while singing, should be higher, rather than lower, as is the current, though erroneously point of view.*

It is critically important, with all these forthcoming ascending exercises, that the singer apply the fully open throat o (oh) then threading the open a (ah) vowel through it, for all of the scales. Imposing the open o (oh) vowel's throat-position on the a (ah) vowel in this manner helps the singer to maintain the "roundness" of throat-position, with a free flowing breath-force, mandatory for performing all vocal movement, up and down the complete vocal range, and *free and liquid* for the entire duration of a selected ascending scale. But if the singer senses that too much roundness of tone has occurred, making his voice stiff, he should stop applying the o (oh) vowel, and use the AW vowel sound, until all rigidity has been eradicated.

Figure 1

hollow
u (oo)

The exercises of *Figure #1 (*above*)* employ wide-spaced intervals which demand that the singer perform a modified version of the swelled-tone exercise. The singer establishes the first note with a *p* dynamic, then ascends to the top note of the scale with it, retaining as much of the soft dynamic as possible. Upon arriving at the top note, the singer quickly swells the tone to the *ff* dynamic, sustains the tone for as long as it is comfortable, to evaluate its intonation and vowel purity, then descends to the lower note, at the same *p* dynamic with which the lower note was first sung. The open i (ee) vowel *(accompanied by a free flow of the breath stream),* should be used for these first ascending exercises, arrived at by threading it through the throat space of the hollow u (oo) vowel.

Figure 2

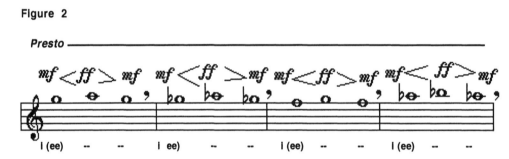

The exercises of *Fig. 2* (*above*) may seem extremely high in the vocal range to perform, *so early* in the warm-up session. However, understand, they are structured as a means to avoid the mistake of *"grabbing"* excess chest voice weight, from the middle range, middle C to the Fn above it. If this negative "grabbing occurs" the singer will immediately realize that fact because it will stop the breath flow. The other advantage of the exercises is that, with this rapid approach, it is more likely that, the singer will correctly engage more of the upper register's muscular control, than lower register muscular control.

Figure 3

The exercises of *Figure 3* are structured so as to bring all the tones from middle C, upward, into a closer interrelationship with each other.

Anthony Frisell—104

Each of the above exercises employ an advantageous combination of:

1) The open i (ee) vowel, when always evoked with a free flow of breath.

2) The *ff* dynamic, and,

3) Swift execution, so as to thrust the singer into rapidly coupling the head and chest voice's muscular actions together, and discovering the purest and most spontaneous interrelationship between them possible. When the purest coupling of the two registers has been correctly achieved in this range area, it serves as a model of how the power of the chest voice is to be correctly connected to the remaining lower tones of the tenor's range.

With the first tones of the exercises of both *Figures 1 and 2*, the singer must direct all the energy of the breath force, demanded by the ascending scale upward and backward, behind both the soft and hard palates. As the singer ascends to the top note of the exercise, he must curve the open i (ee) vowel further backward and upward, toward the head cavities and the tone's proper focal point.

With the exercises of *Figures 1 and 2*, the remaining vowels of *the open e (eh), o (oh), and (ah) vowels* may be tried, but it is better to wait until after having performed the next set of exercises.

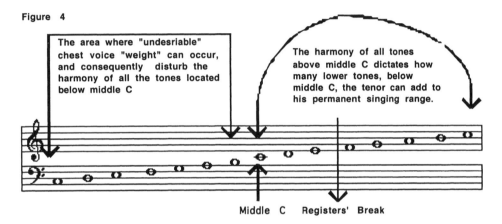

Figure 4. It is critical for all tenors, *" lyric", "spinto" and "dramatic",* to understand the importance of achieving muscular harmony from middle C upward, before deciding how many tones, below middle C, they can added to their "permanent" singing range. The upper area of the tenor voice, and the region of the registers' break, serve as a mirror for the remaining lower tones of the tenor's range. When the tones of the registers' break function properly, it is probable that all other tones of the range will function properly as well. When the lower range of a tenor becomes *"overloaded"* by the *"weight"* and" *thickness"* of too many low notes, the muscular harmony of the *middle and upper range* suffer. Then some of these lower tones must be eliminated.

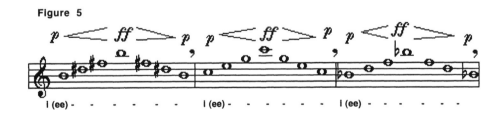

The exercises in *Figure 5* *"gather"* all the tones of the tenor's range very closely together. The ability to correctly perform these exercises *accomplishes and defines* for the singer the ideal muscular harmony which must be structurally achieved. Since each exercise of *Figure 5* requires a *ff* dynamic *(breath energy force near its peak)*, and there is little margin for error. The first tone of each scale is critical to the success of the exercise, therefore, each first tone must be totally dominated by the muscular controls of the advanced developed falsetto, or *"mixed voice"*, but not exclude the chest voice.

The *focal point* of each *first tone* must be tilted upward and backward in the throat, "pointing" toward the three upper notes of the pattern. If any of these first tones—specifically, the bottom B♭, B♮ or middle C—are improperly sung (without the mixed-voice), there is no possibility of the singer achieving success with these scales. As the singer sings each successive rising tone of the scale, he must "focus" its vital energy backward and upward behind the soft and hard palates, purposely "curving" the entire scale in a vertical, curving ascending line which is similar to the inner circle of the letter " C ".

When the negative power of the chest voice *(tones produced without the cooperation of the mixed voice)* incorrectly controls any of these first notes, there is *no* possibility for the singer to add the positive power of the chest voice *(power "mixed" with and dominated by the developed falsetto voice and which is "transportable")*, to all notes of each scale.

Unless all tones of the exercises of *Figure 5* are totally dominated by the *mixed voice* mechanism of control, the dynamic energy demanded by them will immediately deny the singer a smooth passage from the first note to the upper notes, and then the descent. If the singer finds that he cannot sing the starting note of each scale properly, with total head voice dominance, then he should *not attempt* any of these scales. When this is the case, it usually indicates that the tones located just below middle C need further head voice influence.

If the singer experiences difficulty in performing the exercises of *Figure 5,* he should consider that other structural deficiencies may exist. The tones below middle C may not yet be sufficiently developed with the detached falsetto, so as to grant him the use of the *mixed voice*. If any of the lower tones are weighed down with the negative power of the chest voice, the singer should structurally correct this deficiency. This can be accomplished by performing many descending scales with the "detached falsetto", to overlap all the *chest* tones.

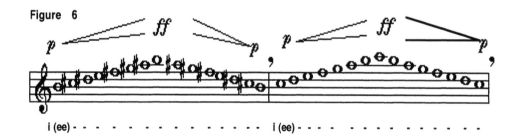

Figure 6

i (ee) - - - - - - - - - - - - - i (ee) - - - - - - - - - - - -

With the scales of Figure 6 and 7, the singer is presented with some extended ascending scales whose tones lie in very close proximity to each other. These exercises embrace the most important tones of the tenor's vocal range. The singer should *only* perform these exercises when there is no negative chest voice weight or bulk with any tones of the lower half of the scale.

These scales should be performed with near maximum volume It is critical that the singer direct these scales backward and upward toward the posterior area of

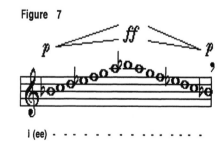

Figure 7

i (ee) - - - - - - - - - - - - - -

his throat, and behind both the soft and hard palates, following the curved, vertical ascending line of the vocal tract. When successfully performed, the exercises of *Figures 1 through 7* establish a taut, dynamic, harmonious relationship with each other. However, the singer must always insure that the head voice's muscular controls of these scales dominate the tones of the lower range.

There is a basic principle to consider, when the singer adds more lower tones to his range. It is that the upper octave's dominance over the entire range will accurately help him decide whatever and new lower notes, at all, can be added to his permanent range. If the singer has mistakenly added a new, questionable low note to his range *(when the tones of the passaggio and the tones above it are already relating in a muscularly harmonious manner)*, the muscles of the throat would reject the new, doubtful lower note. The throat muscles would refuse the singer correct usage of the *passaggio*, and the tones above it. When this is the case, the tenor must eliminate any *new* lower notes he has added to the lower part of the range, making evaluations as he proceeds. This will return the tones of middle C to E♮ to their state of muscular harmony.

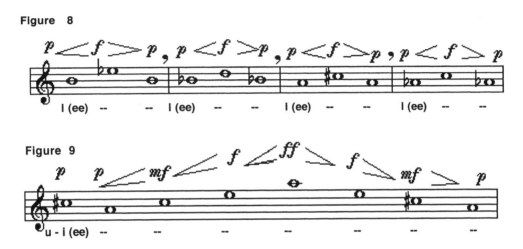

Figure 8

I (ee) -- -- I (ee) -- -- I (ee) -- -- I (ee) -- --

Figure 9

u - i (ee) -- -- -- -- -- -- --

With *Figure 8* we present some exercises which cautiously add bottom tones, below middle C, to the "vocal platform tones" *(middle C to the E♮ above it)*. The keys of the exercises may be lowered *(by half tones)* so as to include as many lower tones below middle C as is comfortable, with the idea of maintaining harmony of the tones of the *passaggio*.

With *Figure 9*, we present a new, extensive ascending scale exercise. The first tone requires that a hollow u (oh) vowel be established, then the singer must pass the open i (ee) vowel through it's center, then use the throat position of the open i (ee) vowel for all the remaining notes of the scale. Breath tension, in the form of a a free flowing stream, must be applied to each successively higher tone of the exercise, in the manner prescribed by the *esclamazio languida* exercise *(p. 131)*

To apply the breath tension dynamics of the *esclamazio languida* to the scale of *Figure 9*, the singer establishes a *p* dynamic with the *1st tone* and descends the scale with this same *p* dynamic, to the *2nd tone*. When ascending to the *3rd tone*, the singer momentarily reduces the volume, then gradually increases the volume of the *3rd tone,* until the *4th tone* is reached, where the *f* dynamic must be established. Upon leaving this *4th* tone, the singer momentarily reduces the volume and ascends toward the *5th tone*, gradually increasing the volume to the maximum dynamic of *ff*. Once the top note has been accomplished, the singer must descend the scale without taking a new breath. To accomplish a smooth descending scale, the singer applies all there breath tension dynamics in reverse order. It is very important to remember that the upward and downward movement of any scale must follow the *posterior-vertical pathway,* as though moving along the inner circle of the letter *"C"*.

Figure 10

u (oo)- i (ee) --   --   --   --   --   --   --   --   --   --   --   --   --

With *Figure #10* we have an extensive, ascending scale in which the notes are positioned in close proximity to each other. The open i (ee) vowel is best for revealing to the singer the precise "throat position" of each tone in relationship to all neighboring tones. The open i (ee) vowel is the perfect tool for guiding the correct direction of the curving ascending scale, taking each successive tone correctly along the passageway of the vertical ascent.

If the open i (ee) vowel is not tuned to the same throat-socket as the hollow o (oh) vowel, it will tend to break away from the correct posterior pathway of the vertical ascent, and refocus itself incorrectly forward into the front of the mouth cavity. The open i (ee) vowel helps each tone of the scale to avoid breaking away from its neighboring tone and tilting in wrong directions that would disrupt the strict alignment of all the tones of the scale. The correct open i (ee) vowel allows the singer to *"skewer"* each tone of an extended scale through the center of its throat socket, thereby revealing to the singer each tone's precise focal point. The exercise should be performed in higher and lower keys, to incorporate as many tones of the vocal range as is comfortably possible.

The dynamics of the *esclamazio languida*

The hollow o (oh) vowel, and the open i (ee) vowel, after it has been passed through the open o (oh) vowel, have been assigned to the exercises of *Figures 11& 12.*

Figure   11

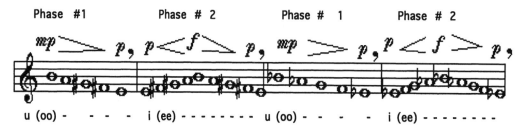

| Phase #1 | Phase # 2 | Phase # 1 | Phase # 2 |

u (oo) -   -   -   - i (ee) - - - - - - - u (oo) -   -   -   - i (ee) - - - - - - -

Figure 12

Each exercise of *Figures 11 and 12 (above)* are to be performed in two separate phases. *Phase 1* uses the hollow o (oh) vowel exclusively, in a descending direction, with all tones, dominated by the muscular controls of the advanced *falsetto* mechanism. In *Phase 2,* the use of the open i (ee) vowel, when it has been passed through the hollow o (oh) vowel, automatically adds both the bright core of the chest voice and the correct focal point to each tone. And the ascending direction of the scale adds even more chest voice. It is therefore important that the singer preserve *50%* of each tone's falsetto muscular control. So, each tone functions with 50% head voice control and *50%* chest voice control, with both muscular systems' controls merging.

The singer must eventually apply the open e (eh), the open o (oh), and the fully open throat a (ah) vowels. Applying these open vowels, at this stage of development, is of major importance. This is so because with the continued use of the closed vowels *(necessary to advance the participation of the advanced falsetto throughout the range),* the singer's voice could readily become *"sluggish" and "unresponsive".* The use of the open o (oh) and the open a (ah) vowels *(if not applied to extreme)* will return the vital core brilliance of the chest voice and the necessary sense of "open throat".

When tenors perform the exercises of *Figures 11 and 12*, they must be mindful of the dangers involved in singing the lower tones of the tenor range. Tenors must avoid making contact with the raw muscular action of the chest voice, when it functions without the desired collaboration of the muscular controls of the falsetto voice. This negative action could be unintentionally dragged upward, by an ascending scale, and damage the lower end of the vocal tract. This occurs by improperly neglecting to incorporate the participation of the advanced falsetto muscles, with one or more lower tones.

These exercises may be lowered a half tone or two, to encompass as many correctly structured lower tones as is possible. However, it should be noted that to include too many lower notes could be disruptive to the harmonious function of the tones of the registers' break. It is not unusual for many *"heavy voice"* tenors to be wrongly classified as baritones. When this is the case, the development of the muscles of the chest voice has been exaggerated and the muscles of the *falsetto* neglected. If it is decided that the true classification is *that of tenor*, then the muscles of the head voice must be given preferential treatment. Once the muscles of the chest voice have dominated a tone, or group of tones, for a long period of time, the chest voice will not easily relinquish its dominance over those tones to the head voice.

Figure 13

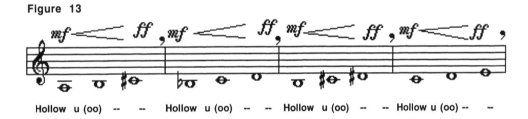

In such an instance, the exercises of *Figure 13* will help the singer to remove the dominance of the chest voice from the tones of his lower range, and give the *head voice* muscles a chance to claim them. However, because these exercises use the hollow u (oo) vowel and are extremely low, they can only be used sparingly.

The narrow, highly energized sound "beams" of the upper range

After the antagonistic forces of the registers have been retrained to respond to each other in a harmonious team effort, they still remain forever vulnerable to misuse and abuse. Therefore, the completely structured vocal range must be *continually protected*, and preserved in its ideal state. The most vulnerable area is the registers' break area, located between En and Fn above middle C. Here are some rules which will help the singer to protect these highly vulnerable tones, as well as the rest of the vocal range:

1) The *mixed voice* is always responsible for the greater percentage of the *"work element"* with all the tones of the voice, *but in particular*, with the tones of the *registers' break* area. With the passing of time, and correct use of the singing voice, these *registers' break* tones grow in strength and become capable of producing a great deal of volume used for "dramatic" singing. However, it is to the singer's advantage to sing more "lyrically" than "dramatically" during the earlier years of his career. "Lyric" singing requires a more restrained use of volume than "dramatic singing". When "dramatic singing" is called for, the singer must test the safety of his singing by observing, after having applied "dramatic" volume. If he observes that, each of the registers' break tones can be still reduced in volume then returned to full volume, he may be assured that his *dramatic singing* has caused *no damage*. It is also advisable for the singer to periodically review all the rules which originally brought the tones of the registers' break area to their state of correct function.

2) Each of the registers' break's tones must be permanently tuned so that their *throat positioning is* directed upward, toward the top of the vocal range. The quality and muscular actions of these tones must be permanently "matched" to the developed *falsetto voice, not to the chest voice.* The dominant muscular controls of the advanced *mixed voice* must be continually brought downward, during each and every warm-up session, and made to overlap all the tones of the chest voice.

3) All ascending scales and vocal phrases must be executed in a guarded manner that acknowledges and incorporates the action of the advanced developed *falsetto voice.* The *mixed-voice* mechanism of control must forever subjugate and dominate the negative tendencies of all the chest voice's tones. This is because the chest voice tones are forever ready to *break loose* from the *falsetto's* muscular control, especially when they are performed in an ascending direction, which could cause damage to the vertically ascending pathway of the vocal tract.

4) The critical crossing tones of the registers' break area, *E♭, E♮, F♮, and F♯* above middle C, must be matched in muscular action, quality and strength to the qualities and actions of the upper, falsetto voice, and *not* to the chest voice, for the singer to maintain a smooth transition from one register to the other. These critical tones, for tenors, must be forever sung with their "hookup" points *aimed upward,* toward the upper register's muscular controls, *rather than downward* toward the lower register's muscular controls. Maintaining this critically important, upward focus, will help the singer to avoid the deterioration of the division-point between the two registers. Should any deterioration begin to occur, if not attended to, it will accelerate and eventually cause the two registers to break apart. From that point on, the tendency of each register will be to return to its separate and original "uncoordinated" state. The inherent antagonism which each register held for the other will return to deny the singer superior singing.

In closing

Many young people fail to make a place for themselves in the singing profession not from lack of talent. but through disorganization. The requirements for success are many and each individual has his own particular, personal problems to overcome.

A true desire for success

A major requisite for any achievement is to truly desire the fulfillment of that ambition. The vocal studios of the world are crowded with dilettantes, or "eternal students" who seem to enjoy the routine of preparation for a career, rather than the attainment of it—there is no room for wishful dreaming, for those who truly desire success.

Many are attracted by the *"glamour"* of a singing career, but fail to consider the many *years of hard work and financial expenses that are required.* The glamour period of a singing career *cannot be enjoyed* until after many years of serious training have passed, and even then *there is always more work ahead.* The desire for success must be accompanied by a practical down-to-earth evaluation of one's abilities. To reach the very top of the profession one must possess specialized knowledge and abilities, such as foreign languages, musical training, acting, personal grooming, and business management, and above all—*a reliable vocal technique.* The beginner should understand that, it will take him a long time to reach his goal; *there are no short cuts.* However, if the desire and ability are truly there, each adversity and heartache will carry with it the promise of greater success.

Every individual goes through a major personality transformation before reaching his ultimate goal. With each little success, the transformation gets nearer to completion. The most powerful aid in reaching that goal will be constructive criticism, one's own and those of other. Eventually, the aspiring singer must subject himself to the evaluation of professionals, since family and friends are overly protective and tend to spare the truth. Assuming the full responsibility for a vocal career *is an enormous challenge.* Every beginner needs help. Friends, relatives, teachers, all play a part, but the big test comes when the singer is ready to perform; then the others are left behind and he stands alone. Unwavering confidence must become a part of the singer's philosophy, based upon knowledge of self and true abilities.

Decision and Determination

It has been said that success requires no explanation and failure permits no alibis. Making the right decisions and being courageous and persistent in carrying them out is a great virtue. Many indecisive beginners ask their friends and family, over and over, *"Do you think I can become a professional singer?"* Until the beginner *himself* is confident that he can attain that status, their answers will have little meaning. With certain reservations, if you know what you want you can generally get it; in fact, others will be happy to join your cause by helping.

The habit of indecision goes into professional life and limits growth and scope. Indecision often denies the individual the chance of new and unexpected experiences. *Being persistent is accepting defeat as only temporary,* a state which your next success will change. When we read of some tenor achieving success, it is safe to say that his triumph was gained through persistence. Fame will recognize talent and pay off both in self-gratification and monetary rewards, but *only after* one has shown that he *refuses to quit.*

Inspiration

After all has been said and done, advice given, technique mastered, there still remains an element of power so indescribable that its meaning can only be hinted at. Some call it *inspiration,* but it cannot be explained to any person, unless he already has some inborn sense of its nature. It is sometimes referred to as *"a calling",* also as *a sixth sense* that calls into play the spiritual mysteries of the mind, which have baffled man since his beginning; *it defies description!* It is impossible to describe what goes into the making of a great artist. What seems impossible to the average person is merely difficult to the great. Many singers have been told by the so-called experts, at their initial singing efforts, that they *did not have* what it takes for success; the experts have, more than often, been proven wrong. If you really desire to sing professionally and are prepared to make the necessary sacrifices to do so, then somehow you will; but remember, nothing is free—there is a price for everything. Good luck!

I wish each and every one of my readers success in attaining a superior vocal instrument. The journey toward that goal is long and hard, but—have faith, and never stop trying.

With much affection *Anthony Frisell*

A recent Article by Anthony Frisell

Is there an "American School" of classic voice training?
If so—has it failed American singers?

Hundreds of years after the creation of Grand Opera by the Italians—beginning with an early era of virtuoso singers such as *Pistocchi, Sensino, Crestini, Farinelli, Guadagni*, then broad-jumping forward to more familiar names, *Maurel, Tamagno, De Reszke, Nordica, Melba, Sembrich, Eames, Calvé, Shumann-Heink*, then arriving at the afterglow of a more recent *"golden age of song,"* we had such artists as *Ruffo, Tetrazzini, Galli-Curci, Caruso, Ponselle, Gigli, Lauri-Volpi, Pinza, Rethberg, Tibett, Flagstad, Melchior*, then taking another broad jump in time, we enjoyed the glorious singing of *Bjöerling, Warren, Simionato, Stevens, Milanov, Tebaldi, Tucker, Merill, Peerce, Del Monaco, Treigle, London, Sutherland, Pavarotti, Caballé, Horne* to mention but a few—finally we arrive at 2006 and have to concede that presently, it is almost unanimously acknowledged that there are no singers trained by the "American School" capable of successfully singing the main-stream repertory of Italian Grand Opera, especially the operas of Verdi and Puccini.

After retiring, many famous singers from the above great periods created their own vocal teaching studios and passed down the superior vocal training methods of the old "Italian School," which they themselves had learned. Some of them came to America and taught many outstanding American singers. Then, about the end of the 50s in America, the traditions of the old *"Italian School"* vanished. Was this due to a communication break between the voice teachers of the past and those of the present? Or a revolutionary attitude of arrogance and superiority on the part of a new breed of American voice teachers who emerged after the Second World War? Long after this critical *disconnect* had occurred, echoes of the old Italian School's teaching terms and applications still lingered about in many American voice training studios. The "new" teachers were superficially aware of such *"old school"* principles as *vocal registers, resonance cavities, positions and movements of the tongue and soft palate, low breathing* and *diaphragmatic support*. And some of them bantered them about, to establish their own authority. But they simply didn't believe in their validity and worth, so they swiftly went about creating a new approach to voice training which they believed was "simpler" and "faster." The new school of teachers eventually came to believe that the only sources of the singing voice are the larynx and the vocal cords and that the contributions of the so-called *registers*, the various *resonance cavities,* and the *positions and movements of the tongue and soft palate* were of no importance.

After so many years have passed, we *can't* say for sure that those post World War II teachers did indeed create a new "American School" of voice training. However, when so many American singers auditioning for roles of the mainstream Italian operatic repertory fail technically to qualify to sing them and consistently present similar vocal flaws and mannerisms, we must assume that they were all trained in a manner using similar based principles.

The manner in which the *"new school"* transformed their teaching principles and practices *away from the old Italian School* was to immediately do away with five of the old School's major principles:

1. There exist two distinct and separate vocal registers within the complete range of tones of all singers, male and female, of all vocal categories and more importantly, these two registers are inherently antagonistic toward each other. In order to "produce" a successful singer, these two registers' muscular actions and vocal sounds must be made musically and muscularly compatible.

2. A critically important section of all singers' complete range, known as the *passaggio*—the tones between B♭ below middle C to the G♮ above it—functions radically differently from all other tones of the complete range, and while singing them, the breath's "motor force," necessary to evoke and control these *passaggio* tones, has to be applied in a "different manner" than when singing anywhere else in the range.

3. The singer's *tongue* and *soft palate* play critically important roles with the *passaggio* tones, and their positions and movements determine the success or failure of the singer to control the *passaggio* tones. For example, when the tongue's position is correct, it rises upward and out of the lower throat channel and into the mouth-pharynx cavity, where it arches and imitates the shape of the hard palate, situated just above it. The *soft palate, which serves as a damper*, allows the singer to properly regulate the amount of air flow of the tones from B♭ below middle C, upward to the top of the range and must be made to position itself forward and downward—*not upward*—as is generally and erroneously believed.

4. With every individual tone of the singer's complete range, there exist progressive, muscular adjustments required of the singer in order to accomplish the tone's total fulfillment. These adjustments are implemented as follows:

A) The singer starts a tone which is controlled by the "detached falsetto" voice, and which, if properly evoked, only evokes the *first layer* of vocal cords' participation of the selected tone. This means that the tone is *without* any of the vocal cords' vibrato action.

B) The singer then further intensifies the breath force, and that calls into play the *second layer* of the vocal cords' participation, once known as the "mixed voice," wherein tiny, puffy pulses of the vocal cords' vibratory actions are added to the "starter tone."

C) Finally, the fullest force of breath pressure is added to the tone, and that adds a *third, final layer* of the vocal cords' vibratory action to the tone, which brings the tone to total fulfillment, a condition known technically as the "connected voice, or the performing voice." The terms "detached," "mixed voice" and "full" or "performing voice" were standard teaching, directional terms of the old Italian School, and some of them are still used today by a few voice teachers but without them having the same meaning as in the past. This is so because the new school of teaching did away with the critically important detached falsetto voice, which is the first layer of vocal cords' participation with any tone; which, when further developed, creates the "mixed voice," or second layer of vocal cords' participation, leading to the development of the "third layer of the vocal cords' participation" or the "full voice" or "performing voice".

5. The classic Italian vowels, as pronounced and modified by native Italians, play a major role in correctly accomplishing the above critical factors of superior vocal structuring and singing, and no other language, other than Italian, accomplishes the same superior results. The *passaggio* tones are the most difficult to understand and even more difficult for the singer to solve their physiological, structural needs. These needs can only be structured and properly "placed" into the singer's complete range by strengthening the muscles of the *head voice* register. Briefly stated, this is accomplished by evoking the muscular controls of the top range's tones while *avoiding all contact with chest voice power,* then slowly imposing the *head voice's* muscular controls upon all the tones of the singer's complete range by carrying those controls downward, tone by tone, from the top range downward to the lowest note of the *chest voice.*

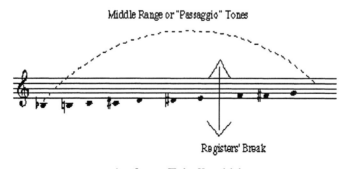

Middle Range or "Passaggio" Tones

Registers' Break

Anthony Frisell—114

The aw vowel, which has completely vanished from present-day teaching, is the best for accomplishing the above. The aw is a combination of the *u (oo), o (oh) and a (ah) vowels*, and it is better than all of the five other vowels, u (oo), i (ee), e (eh), o (oh) and a (ah), because it allows for the greatest, free flow of the breath stream, which is the *motor power* that generates all vocal tones.

Male singers should note that the tones shown in the illustration above represent the *upper middle range* of their voices, while these same tones represent the bottom of *all female singers'* range.

The tedious process of completely resolving the problems of the *passaggio's* tones takes a very long time to accomplish, perhaps *four or five years,* when one knows the proper exercises. In some cases, where the "raw" chest register's power has been forced upward in the range to its top limit at E♮ above middle C, it takes longer, since *the wrong chest voice power* must first be "undone." This is accomplished by applying *seemingly endless,* descending, *detached falsetto scales* to them, with the falsetto form of the u (oo) and i (ee) vowels, then gradually imposing the strengthened head voice muscles' control upon all the tones of the chest voice. The *passaggio's* tones *do not exist* as a separate, muscular, harmonic group until they have been transformed *away from their original state*, into a new arrangement wherein some of their *muscular controls* are drawn from the bottom range and others from the top range. It is comforting to know that structuring the *passaggio's* tones has always been confusing and problematic since the very beginning of man's attempts to understand the nature of and train the singing voice hundreds of years ago. During all past, great periods of vocal training, an experienced teacher knew, from the outset of vocal training, that he/she must never "drive" the power of the chest voice upward in the range as far as the E♮ above middle C. By doing so, it will deny the student the possibility of "making harmonic" the inherent antagonism that exists between the two registers—especially between B♭ below middle C to the G♮ natural situated above it—which is the only way the singer will ever possess a full, smooth and even, complete range of tones from bottom to top.

In direct opposition to the above principle, the new school's dictum was—*do indeed extend the chest register's range upward past middle C to the E♮ above it*! This was not only incorrect, but it was blatantly contrary to historical pedagogic practices. For example, *Manuel Garcia's* table of registration events demonstrates a considerable overlap between the *chest* and *head* registers. All correctly structured tones of the *passaggio* are a creation of *mind, determination, specific knowledge and will*, and lots of time. The superior singing voice *is not* created from the speaking voice, nor is it an extension of it. It is slowly created from an *entirely different set of muscles*, the *head voice group*. The singing voice's muscles are located far above the speaking voice. They are frequently referred to as the *falsetto voice for all males* and the *flute voice* or *whistle voice for all females*. The purest form and applications of these muscles *(free from any and all chest voice)* can only be accessed from the *very top range* of every singer's voice where they perpetually allow the fullest, free-flow of the breath stream. Great skill is necessary in arranging the throat position of the presently sung vowel of any tone, high upward, in the posterior area of the mouth-pharynx cavity, behind the soft and hard palates, which is necessary to enable a full, strong flow of breath, speeding upward from the bottom of the resonance tract, to reach these tones and grant the singer absolute muscular control of them. At the beginning of training, these "hollow," "breathy" *falsetto* or *whistle-voice, top-range-tones,* convey very little of their true worth, nor what finally emerges at advanced levels of training.

William Shakespeare, the famous singer and one of *Lamperti, perè's* best vocal students *(not the famous English playwright),* stated the following in his masterfully written vocal manual *The Art of Singing (Oliver Ditson Company)*: "If, while singing a high note, as softly as possible, *(a detached falsetto tone; author's note)*, and the note is accompanied by a sensation of sound and a full flow of the breath stream reverberating and ringing towards the back of the head, *beyond the last upper teeth,* we shall have discovered the so-called head voice."

Throughout the international singing community, past and present, the *five classic Italian vowels*, *u (oo), i (ee), e (eh), o (oh), and a (ah),* as pronounced by native Italians, have been considered best for training the singing instrument. This is so because the Italian language is essentially free from diphthongs; whereas the most disadvantageous language for training the singing voice is English, as it is presently spoken by native Americans, since it abounds in diphthongs. A pure vowel allows for a specific, single throat position for any selected tone. To the contrary, a tone that employs a diphthong, which toggles between one of its vowels to its other, *does not quickly* "settle down" in the throat to allow the singer to establish a single, specific vowel throat position. This is because the diphthong-factor, being imposed upon a selected tone, confuses the singer as to which of the diphthong's two vowels should be made the dominant vowel of the two, in order to steady the tone's proper throat position *so that pitch accuracy and vowel purity can be resolved.*

A frequently overlooked factor about the classic Italian vowels is that, when they are being taught to English speaking students, they are invariably *filtered* through the sieve of the teacher's American pronunciation of them. Doing this unavoidably alters and misshapen the pure Italian vowels away from their original pure forms, thereby denying the student their Italian benefits. Not only is there a vast difference in the basic sound of each "misshapen" Italian vowel, wrongly pronounced in a flat, dull, strident manner, but there are also vast physical movements of the tongue, lips, and cheeks that accompany the *proper* production of each of the five classic Italian vowels. And, most American *repertory coaches* are also filtering the Italian language through the English language when they endeavor to "correct a student's Italian pronunciation." When that be the case, it stands to reason that the Italian vowels are no longer remotely able to help the singer correctly perform the various vocal exercises necessary to build a superior singing voice, nor to create the same superior "tonal sounds" that result, as when the Italian vowels are being properly produced. It will prove most beneficial for all vocal students if they will apply the classic Italian vowels to their singing voices, exclusively, for at least the *first seven years* of their training.

Here's what *William Shakespeare* had to say about the movements of the *lips, tongue and facial muscles:* While singing: "The command over the expression of the eyes depends upon the freedom of action of the muscles around them; but as these muscles work in sympathy with the muscles which control the face, and which raise the upper lip *(while the vowel being sung properly places the tongue and palate),* all will act free, *if the face is free,* and all will act rigidly, *if the face is rigid.*"

The detached falsetto versions of the i (ee) and e (eh) vowels help the singer to understand the "lift up" principle. The "lift up" involves certain movements of the lips, cheeks and tongue which elevate the entire upper section of the range (for all singers) away from the entire bottom section of the range, starting at C♯ above middle C upward, for all male singers, and C♯2 and upward, for all female singers, to the very top of the range.

Accomplishing the "lift up" while exercising the voice or while singing enables the singer to maintain muscular harmony and balance between the upper *dominant area* of the complete vocal range and the lower *subordinate area* of the complete range by subordinating, as the singer ascends the range, all negative aspects of the lower range, such as inappropriate bulk and weight, upon arriving at the critical C♯ for male singers, and C♯2 for all female singers. The "lift up" principle is a very important factor for achieving superior singing. Present-day training principles do not consider the "lift up" but oppose its critically important principles by applying exercises that create a rigid jaw and restrictive movements of the lips, cheeks, and tongue. These inappropriate vocal exercises quickly and undeniably create a permanent antagonism between the upper and lower areas of the singer's complete range. This forces all singers, whose training *excludes* the important *"lift up"* principle, to almost totally negate the bottom area from their complete range.

When advanced American vocal students begin to audition for their first operatic roles, they are frequently required to present several vocal selections *in various foreign languages*, usually Italian, French, German, Russian, and sometimes English. Nothing shows more *ignorance,* on the part of those individuals holding these auditions, of the true nature of a superior singing instrument, nor its structural requirements, where "language-influence" is concerned. By them requiring this damaging audition-policy, it also shows a lack of consideration for the singers' voices.

Italian operas were composed in Italian, to be sung by Italian speaking singers—essentially, *all Italian operas are dramatic.* These Italian opera composers sought out "dramatic" stories that presented them with a full range of human experiences: sorrow, joy, happiness, success, tragedy, betrayal, and almost always, in the end, they ended with death. The music which these Italians composed for these dramatic operas had to fulfill the high peaks and low valleys of human emotions. These dramatic operas required exceptional singers who can sing with a full range of dynamics and a large variety of vocal timbres: sad, happy, angry, surprised, joyful, betrayed, disappointed, passionate and loving. Those singers who could bring the Italian composer's scores to life possessed superior vocal techniques. To make a point, how could any soprano, when singing Puccini's Tosca, in the second act, after Tosca has murdered Scarpia, fulfill the dramatic moment that Puccini intended *if she does not* possess a *mixed chest register* for Tosca's declamation: *"E avanti a lui tremava tutta Roma!",* like the thrilling *mixed chest voice* of *Zinka Milanov, Claudia Muzio,* or *Renata Tebaldi*?

Surely you have your own favorite moment in one of the great Italian operas, when a certain famous singer sang a phrase in a particular manner that thrilled you to the core of your being and which no other singer thereafter ever accomplished for you in the same way. All superior Italian singers of the past, and some more recently, could sing a full range of tones, all of which possessed brilliance in their centers and velvety roundness around their center; what the early Italian teachers called *chiaroscuro,* "brightness and darkness" combined. A tone with a bright, diamond center with a rim of darkness surrounding it could be sung very softly and sweetly, when that was appropriate, then loudly and "blaring" when that was necessary—tones which were called *squillo,* meaning tones that "blared out" like a trumpet without either extreme of dynamic, loud and/or soft being threatened or eliminated by the other.

It should be noted that, during the student's early period of training, where applications of the five, classic Italian vowels are concerned, there exists a potential for students to produce overly bright or "shrill" tones. Manuel Garcia addressed this issue in his 1840 Paris manual, *Hints on Singing.* He advised one of his pupils *" ...don't be concerned about shrillness of tone in the beginning of training, for it is easily converted away from shrillness, by rounding the vowels."* Meaning that, a voice need not be polished until it arrives at an advanced stage of development. "Rounding the voice" involves certain exercises that utilize the u (oo), o (oh), and <u>aw</u> vowels.

The best American singers, of the past forty years or more, often achieved a certain "roundness" with many of their tones, but in most cases, these tones still lacked brilliance, especially in the bottom range, with *female singers* and in the top range with *male singers*. The cause of this *"timbre-deficient imbalance"* can be traced to the fact that the new school teachers lacked the knowledge as to how to correctly structure the *passaggio,* or passageway's, tones. The dictionary defines a passageway as *a corridor; a narrow track of space, forming a hallway, through which an individual may transit through, in either direction; or a path through which an object, a chair or piano, or what have you, may be transported through.*

If the singer will envision the *passaggio* as being *a narrow corridor* that connects one part of the range to another and which the singer is obliged to send the breath stream into and then through, *in both ascending and descending directions*, the singer will have established a clear cut image of the passaggio. Then the singer may proceed to the problems which cause such difficulties with the *passaggio's* tones.

Rather than to go into all the numerous details necessary to do this *(they can be easily had by reading my manual A Singer's Notebook),* it will prove quicker and more enlightening to explain the two major differences between a singer who possesses a superiorly structured *passaggio and one who possesses a poorly, incompletely structured passaggio.*

Scenario # 1: When a singer possesses a properly structured *passaggio,* he/she can easily sing all its tones with superior tonal quality, pure vowels, and control of all ranges of dynamics <u>because there are no obstacles along the pathway of the complete passaggio which block the air flow.</u> The following facts are critically important. Other than negative effects upon the vocal organs due to illness, which may cause infection and consequential swelling of the vocal organs the two main "blockers" of the passaggio tones' proper function are: *the incorrect positions and movements of the tongue and the soft palate.*

When the tongue and soft palate's movements and positions are correct, they grant the singer free entry for the energized breath stream *(which is the generator of all the passaggio's tones)* into each and every tone of the *passaggio,* then further upward, along the resonance tract, *to the very top notes of the range.* To the beginner, desperately trying to seem naive and too simple and radical an explanation of the *passaggio's* main problems,, but to any advanced singer, these tongue and soft palate factors represent indisputable truth.

Scenario #2: Conversely, when the singer is denied a facile entry into his/her *passaggio tones (which negatively affect his/her top tones),* and is told that the problems of his/her *passaggio* are the incorrect movements and positioning of his/her tongue and soft palate, he/she seldom believes these factors and instead places the blame on other remote, unrealistic and non-related factors for the "blockage" they experience with their passaggio tones.

The critical structural needs of the *passaggio* of most American *male* singers—tenors, baritones, and basses—are generally unknown, *and are seldom properly addressed,* while the student changes from one voice teacher to another in a futile attempt to gain a functional singing voice. No teacher seems to offer them any alternatives to their problems, other than vocal compromises such as: "covering the tone" [a method of holding off the chest voice's brilliance which dulls down the tone(s), and/or "shrinking the volume of the tone(s)]," "humming before singing," "vocalizing with one particular vowel, exclusively," or the most damaging of all, by merely "shouting" the passaggio tones with the hope that they will eventually become musically polished, highly controllable tones.

You may personally experience and thereby understand some of these above negative factors, by going to the back of the auditorium *when the male singers are singing* and focusing your attention upon the variety of inaccurate, unmusical vocal maneuvers and unpleasant tonal timbres which repeatedly occur, with certain tones, along the path of the singer's complete range. The singer's vocal timbres will vary from "dark," "dull," "inaudible," "inferior," "radically open," or "restrictively closed," with severe distortions of the five singing vowels and, in some areas of the range, a few "bright," "clear," "projecting" tones that "hint of professional possibilities, but in general, the singer's efforts present a far-below-standard condition with little promise.

Unfailingly, the male singer's bottom range is barely audible, and most of his tones possess a covered, "smothered" quality. The voice sounds "tired" and "worn." As the singer ascends toward his middle range, the voice grows uncontrollably louder but not better in quality. Control over the dynamics produces "coarse, unmusical shouting." Some lyric tenors avoid these undesirable factors by almost completely negating the brilliance of the chest voice's vibrato with all their tones, from F♮ above middle C *downward to the very bottom of their range,* and by singing excessively softly and sweetly with a soprano-like quality. The Italians derogatorily call these singers *"tenorinos."* They appear to successfully sing the *"bel canto"* lyric repertory for a brief period of time then suddenly vanish, suggesting that something was missing from their voices from the start. Indeed, it was the full collaboration of the chest voice with their exaggeratedly developed head voice muscles!

Every serious singer who places high hopes on someday enjoying a successful, professional singing career should make this infallible, highly revelatory test of his/her voice. Make a recording of one of your best sung arias, one that you feel best demonstrates and justifies why you should be hired by a major operatic theater manager to sing an operatic role for a two or three-thousand member audience of opera lovers. Then make a second recording, placing your best sung vocal selection next to *(either before or after)* a recording of one of great singers of the past, singing the same vocal selection as your own. Listen carefully to it over and over before reaching your conclusions. Admittedly, doing this would be frightening, maybe devastating, but it will definitely inform you of your true worth as a singer. During a live performance of an operatic role, if you've "really got it", the audience will burst into enthusiastic applause. If you *don't* have it, they'll applaud politely and sparingly. In some Italian cities, when a singer falls short of the audience's standards, they are "booed" off the stage! Go ahead, find the courage to be your own critically judging audience! This is practically the only occasion when I would recommend to a singer to make a recording of his/her voice, since I believe that doing so, during the long period of training necessary to acquire a great singing technique, is counterproductive.

As far as the purity of the five Italian classic vowels and the manner in which they effect the basic sound of most American male singers' voices are concerned, American singers generally sound *less like the great Italian singers of the past* than do female American singers. This is because, almost unfailingly, most American male singers rely almost exclusively on the speaking voice's vowel sounds and muscular controls to structure their bottom notes, which are the easiest notes of their complete ranges, and to accomplish these "forgeries." For more than five decades now, this mistaken concept—"model your singing voice on your speaking voice"—has *lured* the average American student into falsely believing that the above approach is the only solution to attaining a superior singing voice.

Admittedly, it is much more difficult for *a male student* to achieve a superior singing voice than for a female student. This is because the male singer's total range of tones possess more *chest voice tones* than *head voice tones*, through which most vocal problems find their solutions. Most American male singers' voices lack brilliance and are "hollow" and "foggy" sounding. They sound like an "older singer," who has been singing "heavy repertory" for far too long, even when the singer is young and at the beginning of his training. There also exists a tragically erroneous concept that the singing voices of all singers, as they grow older, thickens and darkens in sound. Huh! That's only the case when the technique is incorrect.

When Garcia perè, during his later years, came to America to sing the role of *the barber*, in Rossini's *Il Barbiere di Siviglia,* the American impresario who had hired Garcia, along with his talented children, because of their "world famous name," knowing well it would draw crowds, was astounded upon first hearing that the "old man's voice" had retained the youthful freshness and beauty of tone of a superior singer, which indeed Garcia was. After completing an extensive tour of many major American cities, Garcia perè and his talented kids returned to Europe, smiling with satisfaction and with their pockets full of American dollars.

Most American female singers structure their voices in quite the opposite way than do their American male counterparts. They generally focus their attention on their top octave's tones and neglect their bottom octave's tones. This is so because all female singers' "true" *passaggio* is located at the bottom of their range, which is so difficult to understand and "fix" and which can be *temporarily* ignored. Even when a female singer can sing with reasonably good sounding tones at the upper middle and top of her range and convinces herself that she has "escaped" all the negative influences of her chest register's "unattractive" and "unladylike," difficult-to-control tones, in reality she has made the same fatal mistake that most American male singers have made *when they neglected the use of their head voice's falsetto tones. Most female singers hold a belief that their voices possess "two passaggios," an upper and lower.* That's OK. *That theory has been treated in great detail, in my vocal manual, A Singer's Notebook.*

Going once again to the back of the auditorium and *listening to a female singer sing,* one immediately observes that their bottom range is weak and almost inaudible, but as the singer ascends toward her *upper middle range,* the basic quality and "pronunciation" of her vowels improve. Then suddenly, the top range "blooms," and the singer takes advantage of her best-of-all singing tones. However, these top tones never possess the true brilliance of *"squillo"* tones, *which blare out over the orchestra and into the audience.* Unfortunately, the early promise of a future successful career eventually wanes, and the voice suddenly and unexplainably fails.

Most American female singers generally sound as if they are singing in some foreign language. However, upon closer scrutiny, one realizes they are attempting to sing in English but instead produce some otherworldly form of Italian or French with a "choked throat" in the lower octave of their range. Once again, a neglected, under-developed *passaggio* is the culprit causing these gross and inhibiting vocal limitations.

The absence of brilliance, of most of the American female singers' lower range, is caused by the tongue and soft palate's faulty positions and movements; both act like *"bathtub plugs"* at the lower and upper entrances to the *true "bottom" passaggio*—at B♭ below middle C up to the G♮ above it—and block the motor force of the breath stream from surging upward from the lungs into the *passaggio,* then further upward in the range toward the middle and top ranges. Once these "plugs" have been removed *(this takes quite a long time),* the *passaggio's tones* and all the remaining top tones of the complete range will gain the much needed, but formerly missing, vocal timbres of brilliance and grant the singer complete control of the breath dynamics and correct formations of the five classic Italian vowels. At their best, most American female singers sound forever juvenile. They seldom achieve the "full," "round," "warm," "womanly" vocal timbres and dynamics necessary to sing the great heroines of the mainstream, dramatic, Italian, operatic repertory.

For nearly forty-five years now, since right after the Second World War, most American singers *have never been presented with the proper methods of utilizing the motor force of breath. That's why* so many American singers, male and female, present little or no timbre variations with their singing and instead sing in a dull, monochromatic, juvenile fashion.

The inherent but wrong pathway of the breath stream, when English is the singer's primary language, directs the breath stream into the mouth-pharynx cavity, then forward toward the lower front teeth; then it exits the mouth cavity, accomplishing none of what is necessary to sing superior tones. The *correct pathway* is backward and upward, in the mouth-pharynx cavity, then behind both the hard and soft palates, and into either the resonance cavities of the sinuses or those of the skull. *All the above is the reason why most American voice students are consistent users of the incorrect and unproductive shallow breathing method,* as opposed to employing *correct,* "low, diaphragmatic breathing."

Admittedly, English-speaking students cannot quickly nor easily *reroute* their "breath stream" onto the correct pathway. This is because the muscular patterns of their tongue, lips, and cheeks, while attempting to sing, *do not* operate in the same manner as when the five classic Italian vowels are operating correctly. *A major talent of all superior singers* is their skill in directing the breath stream into a specific resonance cavity where the assigned pitch is located. This skill can only be perfected when each of the five classical Italian vowels is being properly sung. Each correctly sung Italian vowel positions the upper posterior area of the mouth-pharynx cavity in a precise manner, one which enables the breath stream to flow freely into the desired resonance cavity, appropriate to the assigned pitch; upon arriving within the appropriate resonance cavity, the tone's quality is automatically enhanced and its volume amplified due to the size and shape of the resonance cavity itself, all of which produces a superior tone.

After the singer takes in an exaggerated amount of breath, holds it back, momentarily, within the lungs *(a factor which builds up breath pressure necessary to create a motor force),* then "gradually *releases the breath stream,"* allowing it to whiz toward the vocal cords where it passes through the glottis *(the opening between the vocal cords, the only "door" into and out of the lungs),* then, at that point, the singer must adjust his/her tongue, lips and cheeks in order to adjust the posterior throat position of the assigned vowel and in order to succeed in directing the breath stream into the appropriate resonance cavity. Managing the proper "pronunciation" of the selected Italian vowel *(something radically different than when speaking)* greatly helps the singer to accomplish this task in a smooth and musical manner, employing superior *mental imagery* in an indirect and somewhat unconscious manner.

If all the above *is not* properly accomplished, there is still a possibility of the *inferior* singer producing the intended pitch(es) with a reasonably pure vowel and an acceptable quality; however, *without the fullest potential amount of the breath flow having been properly directed into the appropriate resonance cavity* and then *" focusing the tone"* into the center of the cavity, or the "bull's eye," the effort results in inferior tone. In the old days, the *"bull's eye"* was called the *point d'apui* by the French and the *punto d'appogiare* by the Italians. Setting up this "bull's eye", in its precise place, within any of the resonance cavities, towards which the singer must aim the breath stream, is accomplished by applying various structural exercises using the *head voice's i (ee)* vowel.

The above situation describes the *best* of what could occur when the breath stream is correctly managed; conversely, the *worst* results *will definitely occur* when the breath stream is *improperly* managed. When that happens, the singer, *despite good intentions,* is obliged to "reach away" from the proper controls of the breath stream and instead "grab hold" of the wrong sets of muscles, which produces *"forced resonance,"* as the old Italian teachers described it. Doing so causes the lower jaw to stiffen and *evokes the negative power of the chest voice's muscular control*s which, immediately causes rigidity of all the *passaggio's* tones, resulting in inferior tonal qualities, compromised vowels, and faulty intonations.

Each correctly produced Italian vowel exerts a strong, individual, positive muscular influence on any and all tones of the singer's complete range. The *u (oo), o (oh)* and *a (ah)* vowels group themselves together, and they perform as the "open throat" vowels but to varying degrees of openness. This means that the open or closed manner in which the vowels position the upper posterior area of the throat is progressive. Starting from a *partially open throat position* with the u (oo) vowel, then moving toward a slightly more open throat position with the o (oh) vowel, then finally with the bright, fully open a (ah) vowel, the singer arrives at a fully open throat position.

The *first group* of vowels, *u (oo), o (oh)* and *a (ah),* enables the singer to emit and properly direct the maximum flow of the breath, critically essential to producing all superior tone. Especially useful is the aw vowel which is a combination of the *u (oo), o (oh)* and *a (ah).* These three vowels, plus the aw , are very congenial for producing the maximum amount of breath flow. They help the singer generate free, open-throated, round, vibrant, consistently available tones. However, neither the *u (oo), o (oh)*, nor the *a (ah)* vowels grant the singer *tonal brilliance, vocal focus,* or *precise vocal placement.* Those precious attributes are only acquired through the use of the *head voice versions* of the *i (ee)* and *e (eh)* vowels. In any case, the superior singer, who possesses a near-perfectly structured singing voice, *can sing all five vowels easily and purely* on any and all of the tones of his/her complete range.

The training procedures of the average American student usually rely upon the *u (oo)* and *o (oh)* vowels and a dark, compromised, "covered" a (ah) vowel. There are but few who rely upon the i (ee) and e (eh) vowels to keep their voices going because, very quickly, the initial help of the *incorrect* i (ee) and e (eh) vowels run out of their "tricks." This is because these singers are *employing a wrong version of the i (ee) and e (eh) vowels,* one based exclusively upon *chest register muscular dominance.* Correct and "safe" versions of the *i (ee) and e (eh) vowels* are *the head voice versions of them,* which must be used exclusively to build the voice. Much later, the advanced *head voice* versions of the i (ee) and e (eh) vowels will reveal to the singer the correct manner of singing the i (ee) and e (eh) vowels in the bottom range of the voice by ways of "reflection" and "imitation" of the head voice's muscular actions and tonal timbres.

Generally speaking, the first group of vowels—the u *(oo), o (oh) a (ah)*—produces readily accessible "breathy," "hollow" voices, which *lack* tonal "brilliance" and precise focus, meaning that the tone is not properly directed toward its *center-of-the-bull's-eye* throat position, especially with the singer's top tones. If a singing teacher is aware that the u *(oo), o (oh) and a (ah) vowels* are permanently antagonistic to the i *(ee) and e (eh) vowels* and that each individual group is capable of achieving certain important structural accomplishments, which the other group *can not* accomplish, then he/she is a rare teacher, indeed.

Few students accept the stinging reality that most great singers of the past took *many years* to build their voices to perfection. *Giovanni Sbriglia (1832-1916)* one of the old Italian School's greatest singers/teachers, stated that it took him *nine years* to convert *Jean de Reszke's (1850-1925)* voice from an unsuccessful baritone into one of the greatest tenors of all times. *Emma Calvé (1858-1942),* who *Mathilde Marchesi (1821-1913)* trained to become one of the brightest stars of the Paris Opera, decided that her vocal technique limited her to lyric roles, while she longed to sing the "gutsy" dramatic roles in opera. So ambitious *Calvé* started searching for a teacher who could correctly build her *chest tones, but none was found.* Luckily, she eventually found the great *castrato Dommenico Mustafà* who accomplished her wishes. Mustafà taught her the secrets of correctly structuring her *chest tones* through the use of the *voix mixte (a combination of head voice and chest voice muscular "blendings," applied with an exaggerated breath flow, and certain, little-known vocal exercises, which had granted Mustafà his own great singing voice). Calvé* described *Mustafà's mixed chest tones* as *"certain curious notes...strange, sexless, superhuman, uncanny!"*

A great voice teacher, besides possessing a seemingly endless store of technical knowledge about voice building, plus great skills in applying that knowledge, must also possess superior hearing skills since without them, he/she could not make critical judgments and decisions as to what each individual voice lacks or already possesses and how to go about granting his/her students all their voice's positive needs, while eliminating all their faults.

F. Husler, the famous German voice teacher of *Leoni Ryseneck, Sàndor Kónya,* and soprano *Karen Bransen,* all of the Metropolitan Opera, had much to say about the teacher's hearing: *"We no longer have at our disposal the acute sense of hearing once possessed by great teachers of singing of the past. . . Our ears have lost that strange kind of intuitive, almost somnambulistic intelligence, together with its extraordinary, accurate, discriminating faculty."*

Sàndor Kónya studied with me for the last seven and a half years of his Metropolitan Opera career, and *Karen Bransen,* also of *"the Met,"* for about two years. *I did not teach Leoni Ryseneck.* I also taught Metropolitan tenor *Flaviano Labó* off and on, for approximately two years. Since he was so successful, he had to frequently leave town for an engagement with one or more of the great opera houses of the world. Of course it must be acknowledged that before working with me, Mr. Labó had already studied with several illustrious voice teachers, such as *Gina Cigna, Carmen Melis, Apollo Grandforte, and Ettore Campogallilani.*

But voice training *is not* a solo act—it is a collaboration, and each superior teacher requires a superior student in order to produce a great singer. *But where is such a rare creature during these unusual, troubled, financially strained times?* Most present-day students are ill-prepared for the long, testy course of vocal training that a superior teacher would lay out before him/her, especially when the amount of time needed to complete it varies from individual to individual and is unpredictable at the start of training.

In closing, and in fairness to the dismal picture that I've presented about the so-called "New American School of Voice Training," I'd like to add that presently, in Italy, Italian voice teachers *are not* doing much better than American voice teachers with their production of great "Italian voices" as in the past. Most of their professional singers sing with strident tones that lack "roundness" and "beauty," resulting from one of the *possible negative influences of the Italian language, which is prone to extreme "openness" if not modified by "rounding."*

It is not surprising that most young, hopeful European and Asian voice students are flocking to America for their voice training. However, they are unfortunately basing their decision to come here upon the "canned" singing they've heard on popular American CDs where often the singers' voices have been enhanced by advanced audio techniques, to give them whatever they lack, but all of which would be immediately revealed and recognized if the same singers were heard performing "live" in any major theater.

During the long, testy, tedious process of obtaining a superior singing voice, the "organs" of the singing voice are being transformed away from their inherent behavior, toward new muscular patterns and responses appropriate for the singer to sing demanding vocal music, which is as much an athletic feat as a mental and esthetic one. At the very end of training when the superior singing voice has finally been obtained, and while singing, the vocal organs behave radically different than they once did at the start of training. They *must not* be made to return to serving the old speaking voice! Doing so would throw them out of harmonious balance with each other. It is for that reason that great singers usually adopt a rigid, permanent policy of *limited, soft volume speaking.*

Most American vocal students greatly resist the transformation of their singing organs away from the muscular patterns of their speaking voices and only feel comfortable when their larynx is incorrectly mired in its lowest, immobile position, whereas the larynx must always be free to adjust to the various positions necessary to satisfy accurate intonation and pure vowels. Frequently, after their voice lessons, and *sometimes during a voice lesson*, American students feel that the arrangements of their vocal organs are strange, uncomfortable, disorienting. Because of this, they mistakenly attempt to return the vocal organs to their old, speaking voice's muscular positions and responses. This is both foolish and counterproductive. The serious singer must acknowledge that they can't have the situation both ways—a speaking voice that is available for hours on end for unimportant, daily chatter—or a great, sensitive, beautiful and guarded singing voice that is capable of bringing one of the great operatic masterpieces to life.

If any of my readers truly believe that the vocal organs of a great, professional singer are aligned and related to each other in the same manner as the speaking voice and that the speaking voices' muscular arrangements are capable of permitting the singer to sing a challenging operatic aria, accompanied by a full orchestra, then he/she is living in *"Lollypop Land"* and has never been anywhere close by a great opera singer while he/she is singing a physically demanding operatic aria. Admittedly, there is much more to vocal training than all the above. If the reader wishes to learn more about my own teaching theories and practices, he/she may read one of my many published vocal manuals. For a start, I suggest *A Singer's Notebook* and *The Art of Singing on the Breath Flow,* which can be purchased through *Patelson's Music House, 160 West 56th Street, in Manhattan, NY. Tel: 212-757-5587.*

Thank you very much for your interest and patience. Always keep in mind that I am a sincere and faithful friend of the singer and very sympathetic to his/her outrageously challenging plight! Therefore, I close with a fantasy-dream about a coming vocal-teaching revolution, followed by a *renaissance* of the great training techniques of classical singing that produce great singers. I'm presently searching for allies to bring that *renaissance* about. So, get serious and do join me in the cause.

With best wises and much affection, Anthony Frisell— April 2006, New York City

Anthony Frisell

Anthony Frisell was born in New Orleans, Louisiana, of Italian immigrant parents. He first encountered the world of opera through recordings, and would often debate with his boyhood friends about the merits of *Beniamino Gigli* versus *Jussi Bjöerling*. After high school, Frisell studied singing briefly in New York City before returning to New Orleans to take up stage directing with the *New Orleans Opera Company*. There he worked with conductor *Walter Herbert* and *William Wymetal,* and such great singers as *Richard Tucker, Leonard Warren, Jan Peerce, Dorothy Kirsten, Mario del Monaco, Robert Merrill, Victoria de los Angeles, and Zinka Milanov.*

Mr. Frisell returned to singing for three years under the guidance of *Giovanni Cacetti*, a wealthy opera enthusiast who was the first to introduce Frisell to the "head voice" theories of voice training. Following a brief career as an operatic tenor in Italy, Mr. Frisell returned to New York and developed a school of voice training that resulted in the publication of his first voice book, *The Tenor Voice*. This was followed by *The Soprano Voice* and *The Baritone Voice,* all of which have remained in print and are very popular throughout the world. He has taught many international opera stars. He has since written two more vocal manuals, *A Singer's Notebook, 1995, and The Art of Singing on the Breath Flow, 2006.*

He was for seven and a half years, the New York teacher of the great tenor *Sándor Kónya*, and for a short time, tenor *Flaviano Labò,* both formerly of the *Metropolitan Opera*, and many other International Opera Houses. And, for several years, *baritone Seymour Swartzman*, formerly of the *New York State Theater.*

Mr. Frisell initially learned about singing from his years as a stage director, working with great operatic singers on stage. While he acknowledges a particular debt to the extraordinary vocal achievements of both *Bjöerling and Milanov*, it is his work with *Milanov* and her remarkable understanding of singing, especially *pianissimo* singing, that has served as his greatest instruction and inspiration.

Mr. Frisell is also an author of fiction; his novels and many of his short stories have been published in Europe. In 1995, *Golden Throat,* his novel about the international world of grand opera, was published in the United States by Branden Publishing Co. *(Brookline Village, Ma.).* Mr. Frisell has recently written the music and libretto for three operas. His first opera *"The Secret of the painting",* is based upon Oscar Wilde's novel—*The Picture Of Dorian Gray.* His second opera *"Rasputin"*, is based upon the lives of *Rasputin* and the *Romanovs* of 1917 revolutionary Russia. His third opera, *La Vendetta,* is based upon one of his own, original short stories, of the same name.

Master Classes

given by

Anthony Frisell

Mr. Frisell is available to conduct master classes. He may be contacted in
New York City, at (212) 246-3385